DESTINY

FROM SHOESHINE BOY TO MAYOR

Norman Ciment

Ktav Publishing House

Urim Publications

Destiny:
From Shoeshine Boy to Mayor

by Norman Ciment

Copyright © 2024 Norman Ciment

Typeset by Juliet Tresgallo

Printed in Israel

First Edition

ISBN 978-965-524-378-9

Cover design by the Virtual Paintbrush

KTAV Publishing House
527 Empire Boulevard
Brooklyn, NY 11225
www.ktav.com

Urim Publications
P.O. Box 52287
Jerusalem 9152102 Israel
www.UrimPublications.com

Cataloging-in-Publication data is available from the Library of Congress.

PRAISE FOR *DESTINY*

"Blessed with a keen intellect and broad vision, Norman Ciment used his gifted civic and communal leadership qualities to develop a vibrant community on the white sands of Miami Beach. His deep passion for Jewish education and culture inspired the growth of the Hebrew Academy of Greater Miami, of which he served as president for many years."

– RABBI SHRAGA GROSS, Former Principal of the Hebrew Academy and Rav of Netivei Hatorah, Beit Shemesh

"To say that Norman Ciment was a 'trailblazer' would be to say that Martin Luther King Jr. was just good for civil rights. His charitable endeavors (in the U.S. and Israel) are legendary. When I think of this outstanding human being, I am reminded of the famous words of Winston Churchill who said, 'We make a living by what we get, but we make a life by what we give.' The author of this book, Norman Ciment, epitomizes this philosophy."

– JUDGE ROBERT GROVER

"Mayor Norman Ciment is a dynamic leader and one of the earliest supporters of the Simon Wiesenthal Center. He understood very well that, despite the Allied victory over Hitler, antisemitism and bigotry had crossed the Atlantic and had to be confronted and challenged. He admired Simon Wiesenthal and accepted his warning that 'freedom is not a gift from heaven but must be fought for each and every day.'"

– RABBI MARVIN HIER, Founder and Dean Emeritus
of the Simon Wiesenthal Center and Co-chairman
of the Museum of Tolerance Jerusalem

"Judge Ciment's recognized intellect and *rochmonis* are at the root of his creative philanthropy, commitment to Jewish education, and his professional accomplishments as an attorney, Judge, and mediator. A role model for many, he has made a great impact on people's lives."

– JUDGE ALAN M. KUKER

"For anyone in our generation looking for that blend of inspiration, realness, and a touch of the divine in the everyday hustle, this book hits right in the feels. It's a powerful reminder that with belief and perseverance, you can redefine your own limits. Highly recommend if you're into stories that light a fire under you and make you think bigger."

– MONTANA TUCKER, Singer, Songwriter, Dancer

CONTENTS

Introduction   9

List of Photos   12

The Kick in the Shins   13

The Early Years   17

Shoeshine King of Hunts Point Avenue   22

Mom and Dad   28

Miami Beach   33

College   42

Making the Grade in Graduate School   50

There Are No Coincidences in Europe   57

Seeing the Setup in the Setback   66

The Law Offices of Grover & Ciment   72

Love and Fate   76

Photo Section   80

Political Aspirations   96

Judge   109

Medical Mysteries   112

Destiny and Diamonds   119

Rabbi Gross and the Hebrew Academy 122

Mayor and *Eruv* 124

Brickman and the *Kashrut* Industry 131

Miami Herald 134

Ben Grenald 139

Santa Marta, Colombia 141

Cannes Film Festival 144

Dolphins in New York 147

Simon Wiesenthal 149

Making Real Estate "Real" 151

Mediation 155

Answering Terror 158

Afterword 167

Acknowledgments 171

About the Author 176

INTRODUCTION

Wⁿ HEN IT COMES TO WRITING A MEMOIR, MOST PEOPLE are motivated by different factors. A pop star at the age of 20 might sit down and write out his or her life story and detail what the road to success has been like. A Holocaust survivor might pen his memories, giving over the past to the present, in a subtle reminder that history must be remembered. Or maybe, a person writes his or her memoir as a way of imparting lessons. Lessons learned from a difficult life, or a charmed life, or perhaps a bit of both, depending on the circumstances.

For me, writing a memoir and chronicling the moments in my life that have shaped my over eight decades carry different purposes. On the simplest side, I am writing my story for my children, for my grandchildren, and for my great-grandchildren. In that way, this memoir is personal – fulfilling a need for the generations of my family to know where they came from, who I was to them, and where they stand as keepers of the family. But in a much broader sense, this memoir is more than a family story. More than something that is written in the front page of a Bible as a record for future generations.

This story, though uniquely mine, is written for you.

Perhaps through my story you will also recognize the path that stretches out before you and realize as well that we are all part of something larger. Join me on this journey and experience firsthand the crossroads, the coincidences, and the power of forging a path with the tools that are within your reach and that are handed to you every day.

When looking at the successes and the failures that influence a person's life, there are moments that stand out as turning points. They are the defining crossroads, the decisions that have long-term ramifications and that lead to either success or failure. When I look back on my life, I don't look at those choices as my own doing. I don't think it was my own innovations that gave me success. I was placed in different circumstances, I met different people, and when I was given the opportunity, I ran with what I saw, working until whatever I was handed became a success.

This story is a story about that. It is a story about recognizing the subtle path that stretches out before everyone. It is the story of the people who entered my life and pushed me towards different ballparks, handing me the decision to either hit the ball or leave the field. It is a story of a kid from the Bronx who shined shoes on Hunts Point Ave and sold marbles and cards to other kids on the street to make a few bucks. It is the story of a struggling student in high school, college, and law school. It is the story of a life lived – of struggle and triumph. But most of all, it is a story of recognition that no matter what happens in one's life, there is always a path that stretches out that one usually cannot see until the twists and turns and crossroads are in the past.

My experiences, the situations I have found myself in, and the way in which various scenarios played out in my life tell a story that isn't always guided by my actions as the protagonist in my own life. It takes the gift of retrospect to see that my experiences – though clearly my own – have been guided by something beyond myself. The choices I've made, the places I've been, and the people who have crossed my path have all served greater purposes. In short, many things were just not coincidental.

People flippantly throw around the words fate, destiny, and providence when discussing random moments, but in looking back at my life, it is clear that these forces walked hand in hand with me with every step I took. I thought I was operating on my own, but they were pulling me all along, guiding my choices for my life to unfold in the manner it has.

Norman Ciment, February 2024

LIST OF PHOTOS

With my parents in 1946. I am wearing my first suit.   81

Tepper and I catch a big one, 1961.   82

Joan and me on our wedding day, July 4, 1965.   83

With Jackie Gleason, 1967.   84

Ciment city councilman election campaign ads, 1967.   84

With Rabbi Sender Gross and Abba Eban in 1976.   85

With comic legend Milton Berle, 1978.   85

With my mom and brother Mel, 1979.   86

Running for Mayor, 1981.   87

Election night with my family, November 1981.   88

With Henry Kissinger in 1982.   89

With Dr. Maurice Jaffe, founder of the Great Synagogue in Jerusalem, 1982.   90

With Mayor Ed Koch of New York City, 1982.   91

With Prime Minister Jacques Chirac of France, 1982.   91

With Prime Minister Yitzhak Rabin in 1982.   92

With Marvin Hier (left) and Simon Wiesenthal (center), 1983.   93

With comedian Jackie Mason in 1983.   93

With Ariel Sharon, 1997.   94

Joan and me with Prime Minister Benjamin Netanyahu in 1999.   95

My wonderful family, 2021.   95

THE KICK IN THE SHINS

*M*Y PARENTS MEANT WELL.

Like all other Jewish parents, they wanted their son to get a solid Jewish education. Living in the Bronx, for me that meant Yeshiva Ahavas Torah.

Ahavas Torah was an imposing building with an even more imposing faculty and Rabbi Poupko was no exception: a large man with a formidable beard and *payos* who ran his second-grade classroom with an iron fist clutching a rubber ruler. If a child spoke out of turn or committed some kind of classroom offense, Rabbi Poupko was there, ruler in hand, ready to dole out a fast punishment in the form of a sharp rap on the knuckles. Kids in the class were acutely aware of Rabbi Poupko's prowess, and no doubt so were their parents as children would arrive home swollen-knuckled on an almost daily basis.

At nine years old, I didn't have many options. I came to school dutifully and though I had to deal with Rabbi Poupko every afternoon, there were still some Rabbis in the school who were a bit more gentle. I have fond memories of sitting in Rabbi Katz's classroom, listening to him teach Torah with warmth and love. It was a completely different experience than Rabbi Poupko's harsh, cold room.

On one particular day, I was talking to a friend in the middle of class. We were a rambunctious group, always talking and messing around. Even the threat of the ruler didn't keep us in check. I was sitting at my desk, chatting endlessly, not realizing that Rabbi Poupko was behind me.

Immediately, the ruler lashed out, catching me by surprise on the knuckles. It seemingly came out of nowhere. Usually, I would have time to brace myself whenever the Rabbi marched down the aisle, demanded that I put out my hand, and then administered the corporal punishment while I prematurely flinched. This time, I didn't know the Rabbi was behind me and the unexpected flash of pain was too much.

Back then, the desks were attached to the chairs so in order to get out of your chair you needed to exit on one side. The opening to my desk was directly where Rabbi Poupko was standing when he lashed out at my poor knuckles. However, since I was taken by surprise, I didn't just sit there flinching. Instinctively, I tried to get away and in doing so, turned and kicked the Rabbi directly in the shins.

It happened so fast that I am not sure who was more surprised. My screams from the initial blow soon mixed with the screams from Rabbi Poupko, who dropped his ruler and bent down to caress his wounded leg. In an instant, I imagined the horrible punishment that would be meted out to me for what had happened. Even though I didn't mean to kick him, there was no way I would be able to escape his wrath and I imagined I would be going home with a lot more than just bloody knuckles. I didn't know what to do so I did the only thing any normal nine-year-old would do in that situation: *I ran away.*

It was 20 blocks to my home and I didn't stop once. I ran from that Yeshiva and didn't look back, jumping over potholes and street curbs, dodging newsies and marble games until I was safely back in my apartment.

I'm not sure why my parents didn't march me back to the Yeshiva and insist I apologize, but they didn't. They must have realized that there was no way I could return and so rather than fight it, they enrolled me in the local public school.

In that instant, the trajectory of my entire life changed.

One would think that the sudden move from Yeshiva to public school would send me on the path of becoming irreligious. But the opposite was true. Through everything, I remained faithful to the values I was raised with. I took off my *kippah* and instead donned a sailor hat which I proudly wore each day together with my *tzitzit*. I was known as "that religious kid" and soon made my mark among the other kids in the neighborhood.

I had been a visibly recognizable religious boy, wearing a *kippah* and *tzitzit*. I had been in Yeshiva from 7:30 in the morning until 6:30 at night, protected from the riff-raff and the dangers of the Bronx streets. But as a public school kid, I was suddenly free at 3:00 p.m. every day. I learned the language of the streets, which for a kid my age meant learning how to play marbles and flip cards. I was surrounded by the rough and hardened kids I had previously avoided, pranksters who made fun of my name and would have destroyed the little religious kid I was prior to that "kick." It was a new world for me, a world that opened up my first business ventures and my first exposure to people who were nothing like the kids in Ahavas Torah.

The moment I kicked Rabbi Poupko in the shin, my life changed. At the age of nine, I had no idea of knowing just how much that one action would affect my entire life. But in looking back at that moment, it is clear that there was something more at play.

I would never kick a teacher, much less a man like Rabbi Poupko who held such a formidable shadow over my every day. I don't know what happened. It was as if another force created the perfect storm for me to try and leave my seat and at that exact moment directly kick my Rabbi without intention. On the surface, it appears to be a minor incident, but it was a setup for my very future.

One moment. One kick. One action that put me on the streets and taught me lessons I never would have learned sitting in Yeshiva. One inexplicable point in time that in retrospect was a spiritual shove onto the path I was meant to follow.

Sometimes, making a split-second decision turns out for the best, creating small events that translate into larger moments. Sometimes, unintentional actions place you on a path that you never expected to be on, heading in a direction you never planned.

I didn't run away from school that day. I ran toward my destiny.

THE EARLY YEARS

*T*HE BRONX IN 1936 WAS SOMETHING OUT OF A MOVIE. It's been romanticized in films and television shows. There is a charm about it – the tough guys on the streets, the small apartments, the kids running around and sitting on door stoops late into the summer evenings. But experiencing the Bronx in the 1940s was anything but romantic and nostalgic.

The block I grew up on was filled with cookie-cutter apartment buildings, rising out of the concrete. There were around 100 apartments in each building, inhabited by families like my own, struggling to get by, working hard, and barely making it. As a child, I grew up speaking only Yiddish. My mother even told me that one day, after going outside to play with some neighborhood kids, I asked her what language they were speaking. Turned out, they were just speaking English.

My life in New York was surrounded by family. Every Saturday afternoon, my parents, Regina and Jack, my brother Mel, and I would visit my grandparents. My uncles Louis, Leo, and Morris would come as well with their friends and their children. My aunt Sadie, my father's sister, would also join us. I would spend time with my cousins and eat my grandmother's food. She always had cake and candy for us. The day was like a large party. On Sundays, we would visit my other grandparents on the East Side. Again, it was a day filled with cousins, food, and good times.

I'll never forget when my grandmother took me shopping for a suit.

The shopping district on New York City's Lower East Side in 1945 was a labyrinth of narrow, crowded streets lined with charming brick and stone buildings. Here, the tapestry of life was woven together by a diverse population, each contributing to the unique character of the district.

Food markets, teeming with the freshest produce, tantalizing spices, and flavors from far-flung corners of the globe, stood alongside delicatessens and bakeries beckoning with the aroma of traditional Jewish fare, offering bagels, challah, and the mouthwatering allure of pastrami sandwiches. The streets echoed with the clatter of pushcarts, each vendor vying for attention with their array of goods, from household items to exotic spices and crafts.

My mother had asked my grandmother to take me there for the suit. I was nine years old at the time and I walked with my grandmother into one of the stores, looking at the clothing while waiting for her to pick the right suit. And then we found it. A perfect suit for me.

My grandmother asked the shop owner for the price and when he said $16, my grandmother didn't even flinch. She offered him $8 instead. I stood there watching them bargain. Eventually, the store owner offered it to my grandmother for $12, but she countered with $9. At that point, they reached an impasse.

"I'm not negotiating any further," he said. "That's my last price."

My grandmother grabbed my hand and said to me, "We have to

leave. He isn't being reasonable." With my hand in hers, we started walking toward the door.

The shopkeeper called us back before we could even open the door.

"Mrs. Moskowitz," he said, "let's try one more time." He looked at me, standing there with my grandmother, and said, "I'll give it to you for $11.50."

My grandmother looked at him for a few seconds and replied, "I see that you are trying. So since you are making an effort, so will I. I'll give you $9.50." They were only apart from each other by $2, but neither of them would budge. So my grandmother, once again, took my hand and started walking toward the door to leave. But this time, when we got to the door, the shopkeeper didn't call us back.

My grandmother looked at me and said, "Tell me. Do you like the suit?"

"Yes, Bubbie. I like the suit," I answered. She took my hand again and we walked out of the store, but this time, we waited outside for a minute. After a minute passed, she opened the door and went back inside.

"Listen," she said, "I came back here one last time, even though your prices are ridiculous, but only because my grandson loves the suit. I'm here because of him, not me. I'll make one final offer of $10."

The storekeeper, without missing a beat, came back and said, "I'm going to make one last offer, not for you, but for your grandson. I'll take $11 for your grandson's suit."

My grandmother bought the suit for the $11, but that one interaction taught me a valuable lesson. She told me, "You need to walk away." But the real lesson was how she shifted her negotiation. When we came back into the store, she wasn't just bargaining for herself, she was bargaining for me. Once I became part of the scenario, the shopkeeper was willing to meet her halfway.

In that one moment, my refugee, *sheitel*-wearing Bubbie, taught me the art of negotiating and how to create a deal, which I used in business and real estate transactions. Again, it is a small point – a tiny interaction that at the time seemed insignificant but resonated for years with every deal and mediation I encountered in my career.

It wasn't just my grandmother who influenced me. During the summers, my entire family rented bungalows in Ferndale or Swan Lake in upstate New York. The bungalows were falling apart, but it made no difference to us. We would eat together in a big hall and spend our days fishing and picking blueberries and apples. My mother would bake pies and buy food from local farmers. It was a beautiful time away from the New York streets for a bit.

My father taught me to sing at the meals on the Sabbath. It was very important to him. At the time, I didn't realize how significant it was that I was singing the songs that came from the shtetls of Europe. That the songs I sang around my father's table were those of my ancestors from Sighet and Satmar.

I spoke to my father about business, even when I was young. He explained that before he was married, his business was worth around $40,000. But the Depression hit and people could not pay their bills. He lived off his equity but eventually lost everything.

Because we had no money, my entertainment options were slim. I could never go to sporting events or baseball games, though by the time I left New York I had an impressive collection of over 500 baseball cards. Unfortunately, I had to leave all of them behind, and I often think about how much those cards would be worth today. But instead of watching sports, I would go to the movies. (Though the way I was able to get in wasn't always legal. We would pay for two tickets, and then once those two boys were in the theater they would open the emergency exit and let four or five more guys in to watch the film.)

Those summers with my extended family, the songs we sang around the table, even my name, "Ciment" – a name that kids made fun of in school and that I begged my mother to change – all of those moments set me up for my successes later in my life. Even speaking Yiddish would one day prove to be a valuable asset.

SHOESHINE KING OF HUNTS POINT AVENUE

---

*T*HE STREETS OF NEW YORK WERE A MASSIVE PLAYGROUND for a nine-year-old kid. The tenements would empty each day, spilling hundreds of kids into the streets. I spent most days playing the games of the time: stickball, punchball, and ringalevio. There were hundreds of kids trading marbles and baseball cards. Some kids took wooden cream cheese boxes, cut holes into them, and created mini arcade games where kids would line up to shoot marbles and try and get them into different-sized holes in the boxes. One could win anywhere from 5 to 20 marbles which, for a kid like me, was the critical currency of my day.

We also flipped baseball cards. That was my strong suit. There were two ways to play. One game was to flip a card and get either heads or tails. If your competitor flipped the card five times and it landed on "heads" then you needed to match that streak in order to win. Another game was to flip the cards against a wall. If you got closest to the wall, you were a winner and you were able to collect everyone else's flipped cards. We would flip three or four cards at a time, and we would play for certain players and team members.

Winning those cards brought you a certain status because everyone wanted complete team sets. I was so good at it that I could flip them against the wall and have the card standing against the wall, which was the best way to win all the cards on the floor. It might seem like fun and games, but this kind of game was serious business. Those cards were valuable to trade, to sell, and to bring personal status to my street world of New York.

My parents, like so many others in the Bronx, struggled to make ends meet. At that time, the money was just a way for me to feel like I fit in with the other kids. There were kids who bought egg creams, ice cream, and candy apples. They were able to buy baseball cards, marbles, yo-yos, and spinning tops. I didn't have any money to buy those things. I couldn't go to the movies. Everything that I wanted required money that my family did not have for me.

I remember one time specifically when I asked my mother for a dime and she refused to give it to me. I was angry, but later that day I came home early from school. We were released early and my mother was not expecting me home at that time. When I came into our apartment, I saw my mother on her hands and knees in the bathroom, scrubbing my father's shirt on an aluminum washboard. There was no air-conditioning in the apartment so she was sweating and disheveled as she worked.

In that one moment, I understood the reason she couldn't give me that dime. My family couldn't even send the clothes out to be cleaned; they couldn't afford to pay for the laundry.

The dime that I so desperately wanted was needed for more important things.

It was an image I would never forget, and I knew my mother was ashamed that I saw her that way – breaking her back to clean my father's clothes, her hair and clothing drenched with sweat. It summed up my entire experience. Even though I was very young, I knew the implication of the moment, and that simple experience of coming in unexpectedly to a scene that I never knew played out daily, stayed with me for the rest of my life.

I could not get a dime from my parents, but I knew that if I had my own money, I could buy more cards and marbles to flip and trade. If I couldn't get the dime from my mother, I would get it some other way.

At that time, there was one ruler of the street: Victor. A year older than me, he was the leader of a group of Italian kids who shined shoes for the commuters traveling by train through Hunts Point Avenue station. Every morning, businessmen and workers from our neighborhood left through that station and returned in the evening. Victor and his gang of five other kids had a monopoly on the shoeshine business, charging three cents a shine on the most crowded spot in the neighborhood.

As the designated shoe-shiner in my family, I knew that I was able to do that well. My job every Friday was to polish my family's shoes for the Sabbath. Watching Victor make money polishing shoes gave me an idea – if he could do it, why couldn't I?

Victor and his gang were older than me and even though we were in the same public school, I wasn't exactly in their friend circle. Apart from the age difference, I was the Jewish kid, and they were Italians. We didn't have much opportunity to socialize. Regardless, I knew that there was money in the shoeshine business and in order to get it I would have to approach Victor's gang and discuss my options.

I mustered up my courage and walked over to Victor. He was the leader of the streets and even though we only had a year difference between us, he loomed large over me. Still, I was undaunted. I knew that he wouldn't let me work with them, and they certainly would not let me set up shop on the same profitable corner. I made him a proposal.

"Look," I said. "I'm not going to compete with you. Whatever you get out of the trolleys and the subways – that's yours. But is it okay if I set up a block away and take whatever is left over?" Even though I was slightly intimidated, I'm sure they didn't feel too threatened by me. After all, I was a scrawny, little nine-year-old.

Victor looked me over and considered my offer. After a few moments, he smiled and said, "Sure, Norm. Do what you want."

I was in business!

I went to the local grocery store and asked them for some empty Philadelphia Cream Cheese boxes. Back then, the cream cheese came in large wooden boxes – boxes that were perfect for launching my own shoeshine business. I fixed up those boxes and found my place a block away from the train station, on the corner of Hunts Point and Seneca Avenue. But while the older kids were charging three cents a shine, I started my business at two cents a shine.

I earned 12 cents that first day and came home to show my earnings to my mother. Here I had asked her for 10 cents, but on my own I earned 2 cents more! When she saw that, my mother scooped me into her arms and hugged me tight. She told me how happy she was and how proud, especially since I had done this completely on my own. I couldn't wait to do it again.

It wasn't a simple business. I spent two hours or so, kneeling on the concrete, shining the shoes of businessmen with a ratty towel that I carried each day. The pavement was rough and my pants barely provided any padding from the stones and rocks that pierced my knees and calves. By the end of the day, my knees were so chaffed and scraped that I had to soothe them at night with Vaseline and warm water. It wasn't much, but it helped a little. I learned to avoid the pain somewhat by bringing towels to place under my knees. It saved me the daily scrapes but was still grueling. Either way, I worked that corner every day, through the pain and the discomfort. I was making my own money – my own dime – and I didn't need to ask my mother for it.

Slowly, after a few weeks, word traveled among the commuters on the train that they could get their shoes shined for a penny less – and it was a better shine at that! I would take the money I earned, including the rare tip, and invest in the things I needed: baseball cards, marbles, yo-yos, and the occasional egg cream. All the things a nine-year-old required to be successful on the street.

Victor and I became friends. He wasn't so concerned about the business I was making with the leftover shoeshine clients because he was so busy on his own block. So even though we were technically in direct competition, it seemed like we each found our unique marketplaces a few blocks from each other and could operate our businesses without stealing from each other. It must have been odd to see us talking together – the little Jewish kid with the tough Italian – but we stayed friends for close to two years. When I eventually left New York at age 11, I gave Victor many of my marbles and my cards, thinking I would probably never see him again.

My shoeshine business was the first of many entrepreneurial experiences that shaped my life, and so in some ways, Victor was my first business associate. I had a good run on Hunts Point Avenue and when I left the neighborhood, I thought I left that moment behind, moving on to new friends and experiences and, of course, new business partners. And in many ways, I did. *But there is always a higher power that controls the seemingly mundane interactions of one's day-to-day life.*

I didn't see Victor again until many years later. Our paths had crossed for one instant on a street corner in the Bronx, a moment in time between an older Italian and a young religious kid. We each went on our way to our own life. I went to law school and became an attorney and started a family.

At a certain point, as an attorney, I found myself in need of some help that brought me back to my old stomping grounds. Working on a particular case, I needed to contact the sheriff's department in Hunts Point to help serve a subpoena. There is a lot of bureaucracy and red tape that makes accomplishing tasks like that difficult and time-consuming. When I reached the office I needed, I asked the name of the person I was going to be connected to. Imagine my surprise when I was told I would have to speak to Victor. My old friend. Before connecting me, the receptionist asked who they should say was calling. I said, "Tell him it's the Jew Boy." Victor soon picked up the phone saying, "Jew Boy? Is that really you?"

Who would have thought that years after shining shoes on the streets, my old friend would come back into my life? It was nothing short of extraordinary.

MOM AND DAD

$\mathcal{M}$Y FATHER HAD TREMENDOUS FORESIGHT IN BUSINESS. He understood the nuances of real estate investing. He built his framing business into a successful company. And he taught valuable lessons to me and my brother.

One of those lessons came from an unexpected place. Every Sabbath, after the meals on Friday night and Saturday lunch, my father would teach us Hebrew songs. These *zemirot* were lively and upbeat songs, some dating back generations, that are traditionally sung around the table in Jewish homes across the globe. My father took the time to teach us these tunes, and it turns out that they helped me in more ways than one.

He never could have known that 40 years after sitting with him at our family table, those songs would help both my business and political career:

I was at a dinner with a group of older Jewish men, all survivors from Europe. All of them were prominent businessmen, many of them were in the real estate industry, and I was hoping to create a connection and maybe sign some of them as clients. I had been invited to join them for Friday night dinner and sure enough, when the meal was finished, they began to sing the familiar songs I knew from my father. At one point the host turned to me and asked me to sing a song that I knew.

The table grew quiet and every eye was on me. I wasn't sure why, but as they looked at me, I felt as if I was being tested by the group.

At the table was the prayer book that everyone used to sing the songs. I opened the book and started to sing one of the tunes my father taught me. It was an ancient melody that my grandfather had taught to him. As soon as the song began, the table erupted in song, all of us singing that same tune.

"Where did you learn this song from?" the host asked.

"From my father."

"Where is your father from?" he continued.

"Sighet, in Romania."

He broke into a huge smile when I said that. Soon the whole table was talking, excited by the singing and the revelation that I was descended from someone in Romania. Three of the men at the table came from the same town as my grandfather. Instantly I became "one of the boys." It was the connection I needed and soon these dinner mates became my clients, forging a trust that was built through the songs I learned at my father's table.

My father's lessons didn't only bring me clients but also established the values that would guide my life. When I was 19, I was sitting on our patio talking to him, discussing a recent framing order that he received. It was a large order from the Disney Corporation for framing thousands of glow-in-the-dark pictures of famous Disney characters. They needed the frames by a particular date, and in order to meet the deadline the factory would have to be open on Saturday. Opening the business on Saturday would have also opened us up to many more orders.

I explained to my father that there are certain ways in which a Jewish business owner could keep his business running on Saturday without actually violating the Torah or breaking the Sabbath. For instance, there is a loophole that a business owner could "sell" his business for the weekend and then "buy it back" at the end of the Sabbath. It was a somewhat questionable way to manipulate the law, but I felt that my father should consider it, especially since it would help the business tremendously.

My father refused.

But we had a conversation that day that has stayed with me my entire life.

We talked about being religious. About believing in God. About observing the Sabbath.

"Staying religious and believing in God shouldn't come at a financial loss," I said. "Besides, we don't even have any proof that God even exists."

His answer to me was simple and logical:

"First, I believe in the Torah and everything that happens in it. Unquestionably. But let's say that at the end of my life, I discover that there is no God. That I was wrong. Isn't it nice that we lived our lives and made time every week to spend 24 hours together, eating, singing, praying, and talking? Isn't that why you get married in the first place? And if, at the end of my life I find out that there is a God – that I was right – then I won twice. I followed His commandments, I kept the Sabbath, and I enjoyed the time with my family. Either way, I am happy."

In the end, we didn't lose the Disney order. My father had his workers commit to adding two hours of overtime during the week and adding a half day of work on Sunday. With that setup, the job could be completed without violating the Sabbath. *It was a powerful lesson for me, one that I remembered every time I was faced with an opportunity to break the Sabbath for financial reasons. I never did.*

My mother's lessons were not voiced in a conversation on the patio but were learned through the actions I observed. She was not educated but had tremendous street smarts and a keen sense of observation. More than anything though, she was a staunch defender of her family and never hesitated to fight or argue in order to protect us. Years later she would defend her grandchildren whenever they were reprimanded. She worked hard. When she was younger she worked in a factory, assembling ties by hand. But she also worked as a janitor, a saleswoman, and eventually a manager of a 10-unit building we owned. She was a master negotiator and was a tough woman if she thought anyone was trying to take advantage of her.

She was also an excellent cook and baker, as were most Hungarian women. I have fond memories of her soups, stuffed cabbage, veal, and goulash. Her strudel and pies were beyond anything I have ever tasted in even the finest restaurants. My children – her grandchildren – still talk about her food and the recipes she shared with them. It's a shame those recipes have been lost as if any bakery or restaurant had them today, the lines of customers would probably circle the block on a daily basis!

But she was deeply caring. I remember at meal times when I was younger, she would look around the table at who had finished eating but still looked hungry. Then, she would get up from the table with her own plate, bring it into the kitchen, and return with her food to offer to my brother or my father, depending on who needed it. I didn't realize until I was older that she was giving away her own food to make sure we were satiated.

My mother also loved to sing and had a beautiful voice. Like my father with the Sabbath *zemirot*, she taught me different songs in Yiddish and Hungarian which I loved to sing with my not-so-beautiful voice. It didn't matter though. In fact, those Yiddish songs, like the *zemirot*, helped me years later when I was running for mayor and campaigning. My old Yiddish songs, sung with my terrible voice, touched the hearts and souls of the people I met. By connecting through ancient tunes, we forged bonds of trust that I never could have fathomed would be built on the simple songs my parents taught me so many years before.

MIAMI BEACH

IN 1947, MY FATHER AND HIS TWO BROTHERS TRAVELED
to Miami Beach intending to move there. My uncles had been
wounded in the war and wanted to live in a warmer climate. Also,
since I was so sick all the time, they felt that it would be better for
my health to leave New York as well.

The first time they visited, Miami was in the middle of one of
the worst heat waves in history. The temperatures soared to 102
degrees and there was no air-conditioning anywhere. My father,
not realizing that the weather was an anomaly, decided to move
to California instead.

It was a short-lived decision. A year later, my father suffered terrible
back pain and an earthquake ripped apart our driveway. My uncle
Leo, who had stayed in Miami through the heat wave, told my
father to move back and my father listened. So less than two years
after moving to California, I headed back across the country to
Miami.

Miami Beach was the complete opposite of New York City. For
one thing, I was living in a private home and would ride my bike
to school. We lived at 127 Meridian Avenue and our synagogue
was on Washington Avenue and 3rd Street. It was a short walk.

There was a police station across the street from us, and since there was no air-conditioning, we would hear the prisoners crying and screaming every night through the open windows. I went to public school, but there was a new day school in the area, the Hebrew Academy, which was in a small building that used to be a church. I was the first boy to celebrate his Bar Mitzvah at the Hebrew Academy. It was 1949 and there were approximately 15 people in attendance. The party was in the living room of our house on Meridian Avenue across from the police station.

It was the closest thing to small-town living. A serious departure from what my life in the Bronx had been like. The father of my classmate Gene Schwartzman owned the local ice cream parlor where I could get a banana split for 29 cents. My father would go to work on a bicycle, and his brother Leo would drive a car dragging a wagon behind him for deliveries. The Galbut family, now famous for real estate and medicine, owned a small hardware store and licensing agency.

Dolly's, a small luncheonette, was located on Espanola Way, which was one block from the school and one block from Washington Avenue where Hebrew National was located. Those were the places where the "elite" guys would hang out to meet girls. On Saturdays and Sundays, though, the place to be was the 14th Street beach. All the kids from North Miami Beach, Miami Beach, and other areas would gather there, meeting each other and socializing. It was everyone's favorite weekend destination.

The social divide was still obvious though. Girls from beyond 41st Street would come in their cars to date the poor kids in South Beach. It was a unique time, and all the South Beach boys established a camaraderie that still exists today with guys who are in their 60s, 70s, 80s, and older.

When I was 14 years old, I worked as a newspaper delivery boy. The job was simple enough, delivering papers around the neighborhood in the afternoon after school, and I earned money daily. It wasn't the most prestigious job, but it was a classic occupation for a kid my age.

During one month, the newspaper I worked for, The Miami Beach Sun, ran a contest for all the delivery boys in an effort to encourage subscriptions. The top seven workers who brought in the most newspaper subscriptions would win a weeklong trip to the Bahamas and Cuba.

This was a prize I wanted!

When the contest was first announced, I tried to get the subscriptions the way everyone else did: I asked my clients, I asked my family, I did everything I could. But very few were interested, despite my cajoling and logical presentations on why they should subscribe. It was difficult to get new customers, and so it seemed impossible to win that prize.

I was working hard. On one Sabbath I was in synagogue, and the Rabbi was running an appeal for a yeshiva in New York. People were donating $5, $10, $18; it was 1950 and that was significant money. My father and my uncle were sitting next to me and jokingly said, "Hey! You're in business. Why don't you make a contribution?"

At the time, I was earning $3.50 a week. I didn't think I would be able to contribute anything, but my father said, "Norman, if you give charity, the money you give will return to you tenfold."

They continued to bother me, and when the usher came to our row I agreed to donate 25 cents. The Rabbi announced my contribution, and the congregation laughed and clapped. After services people came over to me to congratulate me on the donation. I felt like an important person.

I continued to work on getting subscriptions and they started coming in! Additionally, I realized that as I was getting customers, my father's words were coming true. I was getting back my charity tenfold. Years later I learned that my father was also buying subscriptions to prove to me the lesson of giving charity! But I still needed more to win the trip.

I wanted that trip more than anything, and I knew I needed to find a way to make it happen. I had worked hard before to get ahead, and I knew in my heart that I was going to get the subscriptions I needed to win. So I devised a plan with some potential customers. A two-week subscription cost 70 cents. I told my customers that I would cover them for the two-week subscription if they would tell the newspaper that they signed up for a subscription for a year. It was a small loophole that would get me the necessary clients for the contest but also wouldn't require my customers to actually pay for the yearly subscription. In essence, I was investing in my newspaper business to win the trip. My customers agreed and I was set. I waited for the last hour of the contest to give my boss my final list of customers.

It worked.

I moved from 27th place to 6th place and won the Cuba trip. It wasn't a simple win. The boy who was knocked out from 7th place to 8th place couldn't believe what had happened and accused me of cheating. There was arguing and yelling, but I stood firm. Though to be honest, I was a little worried. My boss frantically called all my customers to make sure they were actually customers. I was nervous about what would happen, but all my customers knew exactly what to say. I told them that they may receive a phone call. Sure enough, they vouched for me and said that yes, they were customers of mine. The trip was offered to me.

I can't explain why I wanted to win that trip so badly, but it impacted my life for years. It wasn't just about seeing the country – this was no simple cultural trip – but the connections I made played out in my life later as a lawyer, as a commissioner, and as mayor.

On that trip, I met a photographer named Elarte who owned two stores. My father had been in the picture framing business for years and had sent me with a few samples. Even though I was on a pleasure trip to Cuba, I was focused on business. I walked into Elarte's shop to make him an offer.

Mind you, I didn't speak the language and he didn't speak English well. He had a worker there who tried to interpret for me, but at a certain point, the interpreter became frustrated. Plus, he really didn't want to have to talk to a 14-year-old kid! I knew that I was going to lose this chance and so, without any other means to communicate, I decided to let the frames do the talking.

I pulled the frames out of my bag and showed them to Elarte.

I'm sure he was skeptical, but after I showed him the frames, he was put at ease.

"Listen," I explained, "you don't have to give me the money in advance. I'll send you the frames and if you like them, you'll send me a check. You'll become our customer." The language was still a barrier, but the message came through, especially when he saw the frames and the price.

And that was how I wound up selling picture frames in 1950 to
Elarte.

Nine years after my meeting with him, he escaped from Cuba and
landed in Islamorada, one of the northern Keys in South Florida.
He came with nothing, having left his business behind to escape.
While he knew many people in the Cuban community, the only
people he knew in business were me and my father. He called my
father, and I met him at the Greyhound station to give him money.
Later, we helped him start his business here in America.

If the story ended there, it would be a nice account about business
connections and relationships.

I made a business connection for my father while I was in Cuba,
and it expanded to Florida years later. But that relationship proved
vital to my life in ways I couldn't understand at the age of 14 as I
would find out 15 years later.

I went to Miami Beach Senior High School which, at the time, was
70 percent Jewish. However, I was the only Orthodox student in
my grade level, which was about 200 kids. Money was still an
issue for me. I needed money to buy lunch which I never seemed to
have. So, at the age of 15, I became a "beach boy" working at the
Surfside Plaza Hotel on 24th Street and Collins Avenue. My friend
Warren Tepper was a beach boy at the Traymore Hotel next door.

Even though we worked the same job in different places, Warren
had it a lot easier than I did. He had a pool area to clean while my
job was only on the beach itself. I had to carry lounge chairs and
umbrellas over the sand, set them up, and then store them at the
end of the day. If you've ever dragged anything across sand, you
know how hard that is.

38

In addition, after I had stored everything at the end of the day, I had to pick up all cigarette butts and garbage that littered the beach. The final task at the end of my day was leveling the sand for the morning. I had to take a heavy piece of wood about six feet in length that had an even heavier lead pipe attached to it. The whole apparatus was attached to two ropes that I would have to hold on to, allowing me to drag the entire thing across the sand. I had to do this for the entire length of the hotel beach in order to make the sand look new and pristine for the following day.

In essence, I was a mule, working for $5 a day plus tips.

No one wanted that job, but I needed the money. It also gave me some other opportunities. There were a few bookies in the beach crowds, and I quickly earned their trust. They would allow me to run errands for them, and their customers would give me extra tips. I also worked on weekends as a carhop at night and delivered orders for my father. So between all those jobs, I was making money.

However, with all of the jobs I had, I could not work on the Sabbath. At the beach, I had someone cover for me on Saturdays but that stopped at a certain point, and so I worked for Ben Wasser, a fruit shipping company. Ben Wasser was friends with famous people like Joe Lewis, Frank Sinatra, and other actors. I was a stock boy and a delivery boy but also found different jobs working for Wasser. He had been a manager in a casino in Havana, Cuba, and in addition to the famous people he knew, he was well acquainted with some infamous ones, like Meyer Lansky. I knew how bookies worked from my job at the beach so I was hired to work both jobs.

Interestingly, all of these jobs again became the foundation from where I built myself up. I had learned the basics of working from my days shining shoes in the Bronx, and those small lessons affected my later experiences. I learned early on that I needed to hustle and work harder than everyone else in order to be successful.

In fact, many years after my trip to Cuba, I was working as a lawyer and wanted to sign one of the biggest insurance agencies as a client. The owner of that company was a man named Jesus Rico.

Rico ran his company in Little Havana, a small area in Miami that was populated with mostly Spanish speakers. My partner had previously tried to sign him as a client but was unable to do so. Between the language barrier and Rico's natural suspicion toward American lawyers, it was not likely that he would use us. However, I wanted to try again.

I set up a lunch meeting with Rico and brought an interpreter. The lunch did not go as well as I had hoped. There was a lot of back-and-forth, and while I'd like to think that I'm an effective salesman and my pitch to him was logical and sound, most of my words were literally lost in translation. I was getting frustrated, and I saw that Rico was pretty much finished and preparing to leave when I suddenly had a completely random idea.

"Listen," I said, "when I was 14 years old, I went to Cuba and found a client for my father by the name of Elarte. Ten years later, Elarte came to America and we gave him a loan so he could set up his business. He is one of our best customers. I know you also are from Havana, and so I can't stop thinking that it's almost destined for us to work together."

For a moment I thought I had made a misstep, but instead, he broke into a smile. The mood at the table changed instantly.

"You were the one who saved Elarte? You were the one who lent him the money for his business?"

Rico grabbed his glass and raised it towards me.

"Elarte is one of my closest friends. You and I will be more than just attorney and client. We will be brothers."

Indeed, my relationship with Rico turned out to be more than just business. He was the largest source of new business in my 35 years of practicing law.

Two years after that meeting I ran for the city commission of Miami Beach. At that time, 40 percent of the population was Latin. The person who was integral for me getting the majority of the Latin vote?

Jesus Rico.

COLLEGE

WHEN I GRADUATED FROM BEACH HIGH, I WAS 17 years old and not quite sure where I wanted to go. My grandfather took me to get a blessing from the original Satmar Rebbe, Reb Yoel. That visit changed me tremendously and shifted my entire way of thinking and my attitude toward life.

If you've never heard of the Satmar Rebbe, there are some things you should know. First, it wasn't easy to see him. As the leader of the Satmar sect of Judaism, he was sought after by thousands of people for blessings. People waited three months to get a private audience with him for his advice and his blessings for all sorts of ailments and conditions. All sorts of people lined up to see the Rebbe, including men looking for their *bashert* (the woman they would marry) and fathers with sick children searching for cures and divine intervention. It was not an easy appointment to get.

Seeing him was an emotional, spiritual visit. It wasn't just seeing a Rabbi in a black coat. Sitting with the Satmar Rebbe was meeting with someone who one believed had a direct line to God. He would look at you and close his eyes, concentrating, before coming to an answer. In that moment, you knew you were in the presence of someone much greater than a human being. Even without saying a word the Rebbe created an electric atmosphere of spirituality. It was like nothing I had ever experienced.

My grandfather told the Rebbe that I was the oldest grandchild and that I was going off to college. He asked the Rebbe to give me a blessing for success. After the blessing, the Rebbe turned to my grandfather and asked, "What can I do for you?"

But my grandfather replied, "Nothing, Reb Yoel. I only came for a blessing for my grandson. I don't need anything at all. I am, thank God, satisfied."

I was shocked. At the time, my grandparents were living in a small efficiency and were being supported by three sons who barely made a living for themselves. If anyone needed a blessing, it was my grandfather. And there we were in the presence of a man capable of bestowing blessings upon blessings!

On the way home from the Rabbi's house, we argued over it. I could not understand my grandfather. How could he turn down this chance to get a blessing? It didn't make any sense to me.

His answer was revealing.

"What do I need a blessing for?" he said. "I have health. My children are healthy, I have food on the table. I have a good marriage. What else do I need? I am satisfied with my life."

I started to protest, but he cut me off.

"If God wanted me to have more, he would have given it to me. If he wants me to have more, he will provide it. I am satisfied."

I was 17 years old at the time, and I didn't fully understand it.

Years later, when I was married with three sons, I realized what my grandfather had done. I gave that same blessing to my children at their Bar Mitzvahs. I wished that they would always feel satisfied with what they have and feel safe in the knowledge that if God wanted them to have something, He would provide it. That doesn't mean they should not keep trying to improve, but they should also always, always, remember to be satisfied with what they have.

But when I graduated from Beach High, even before I received that important lesson from my grandfather, I was hit with a real shock. I had spent the majority of high school working, dating, and living day by day. None of my friends had ever spoken about college, and I never even thought to ask. It wasn't until July of the summer after graduation that I overheard kids on the beach discussing the various schools they were going to.

I panicked.

I didn't have any plans. I didn't have any school options. And worse, I hadn't even thought about it!

I went home and discussed the situation with my parents, but they were just as lost as I was. With little choice or knowledge, I contacted every state school. The state schools had lower tuition fees but no kosher food or kosher dormitories.

I decided on the University of Miami, but there was no way they would accept me. My grades were terrible. I was at the very bottom of my graduating class.

I went to the University and applied anyway. I was told that I would be accepted on probation and that I needed to take an exam to help me find what I was good at. The exam came back, and I was told to go to vocational school and become either a plumber or an electrician. But they also said that I could study accounting or finance provided I kept up my grades.

I took that option.

I did well in those classes, and my life changed because of that decision.

I met two people during those early years of college. One was Allen Levine, whom I helped in my accounting class. He worked for a billiards parlor across from the dog track. He did well in the class because of my help and to thank me he invited me to his billiards place on a Saturday night with a tip. I made enough money that night for tuition for the semester. Unfortunately, that night also caused me to lose a lot of money over the next few years!

I also met my Economics Professor George Malanos from Greece.

Every so often a person comes into your life and has an impact that lasts years beyond your first meeting. Professor Malanos was that man. I didn't realize at the time how instrumental he was in setting me on the path toward my success, but I have to admit that my life would have been very different had I not met him.

I was accepted on probation, and one of the classes that was recommended for me to take was economics. I was good with numbers and excelled in math so it was smart to take the classes I would do well in. I needed good grades to get off probation.

But I also knew that I needed to make connections with my teachers and professors. I knew that those connections would help me get ahead and do well. Professor Malanos explained basic economics to me, and in addition made the class an interesting offer. He jokingly said that he builds houses and that if anyone finds him a lot, he would pay him a commission.

He was using it to illustrate a basic principle, but it piqued my interest and I spoke to him after class about it. I wanted to make myself stand out from the other students and thought that this would be the way to do it.

I asked him basic questions about the type of lot he was looking for, how big, what he wanted it for. I wasn't sure if anything would ever pan out, but I wanted to have the conversation with my professor and let him know that I was trying.

I continued his class while also working for my father, and I inquired everywhere if there was anyone selling a lot. I would deliver picture frames all over the city and constantly ask the customers if they knew of anything. Eventually, someone did.

Bill Mesa, a customer of my father's, owned a lot in Coral Gables. I collected all the details and reported back to my professor. I gave Professor Malanos the dimensions and the address of the lot. Sure enough, my professor bought the lot.

After the purchase, he told me how happy he was and that he owed me $1,000. But he didn't have the money right then. I told him not to worry, it was okay, but he insisted on writing out an IOU. He took a piece of paper and wrote that "Norman Ciment is owed $1,000."

I asked him why he did that. I trusted him. I knew he wasn't going anywhere, and he had said that he would give me the money the next day.

"What if I would die?" he explained. "Never leave any business unfinished like that. Always get it in writing and get it signed." At the time, I was focused on getting a good grade more than the $1,000, but he was teaching me a valuable lesson.

It also was the start of our relationship. He took an interest in me and asked me why I was struggling in school, why I wasn't taking a full course load. We spoke and he made some suggestions for me.

"You want to be a businessman," he said, "so you should take real estate law." I didn't really know what I was doing at that point. I took the classes the college told me to take. But here was a professor taking a genuine interest in me and giving me practical guidance.

I took his advice and then went to him throughout my undergraduate years. I took contract and real estate law and other classes, all on his advice. And I did well in those classes. I enjoyed them.

We kept in touch. He spoke to me toward the end of my college years. At that point, we had grown close. I followed his advice, and we spoke about business and classes and my life. It was when he told me to consider taking a few courses in law school that my life changed.

"Work for your father during the day," he said, "and take those classes at night. It will make you a better businessman." I agreed. He knew what I excelled at. He saw talents and skills that others hadn't seen.

I wasn't so serious at that time. I was gambling at the horse track and the dog track, and I was hanging out with fraternity guys. Law school wasn't something on my radar. But because it came from Professor Malanos, I considered it seriously. My father was against the idea. He wanted me to work and certainly didn't want to pay for more schooling. He knew I was not a good student and that

I had lost a lot of money gambling at the dog track. He knew I wasted a lot of time dating instead of studying. More importantly, though, he wanted me to go into the family business. He didn't think I would be successful as an attorney.

I decided to do it anyway.

I signed up for two courses twice a week. I figured it didn't cost me that much money, and it kept me in the college system. I could hang out with my fraternity, gamble at the track, and see the girls I was dating. At the same time, I was taking law school classes.

But this time, I didn't have Professor Malanos to guide me, and my grades in those classes were poor. In all honesty, I was shocked when I saw that I wasn't doing well. I thought I had passed and wasn't sure what I was doing wrong. I decided to discuss it with Professor Malanos.

He looked at my grades and said, "Well, maybe you aren't cut out for this. Maybe you should just drop the classes."

I was embarrassed for myself and worse, I felt like I was letting him down. He had supported me and guided me and now, here he was advising me to drop my classes because I just couldn't hack it. I didn't want to give in to that.

Instead, I decided to try again. I finished the courses and passed them. And because I was still working I decided to take some more classes over the summer.

That was when a transformation came over me. I'm not exactly sure when it happened, or even how, but sometime over that summer, for the first time, I started enjoying my classes and as a result, I started doing well in them. Motivated by Professor Malanos and by my desire not to let him down, I worked hard.

I was working for my father at the time and taking courses at night, but that summer, my father sold his business, leaving me with no choice but to start school full-time – a major decision that caused a huge upheaval in my life. My father, again, was completely against it and refused to support me.

I enrolled in the University of Miami Law School and eventually borrowed money from friends to help pay my expenses. I couldn't live at home, so I moved on campus and spent most of my time studying.

MAKING THE GRADE IN GRADUATE SCHOOL

*S*CHOOL WAS NEVER EASY FOR ME. I WASN'T INTERESTED. I had more important things to do than study. But once I had a goal, nothing would stop me from achieving it, and so, just as I worked my way through college, I also worked my way through law school.

When I was first accepted to the University of Miami, my grades were poor, and I was allowed to matriculate only as a probationary student. I worked hard but found myself in a transitional period for the law school. A new academic dean had arrived from Oxford University with the solitary goal of making UM Law School the Harvard of the South. As a result, he created much higher standards for the classes and instituted new rules for passing classes. Only the top students were able to move on from year to year.

For someone like me, on probation and floundering, this sudden shift in academics was terrifying. I was in direct competition with everyone in my class and needed to stay on top if I was going to survive. If I failed, I had no idea how I would pay back the loans I received from friends. I had no job. No money. My father refused to help me, convinced that I would fail. My mother saw me struggling and tried to help. She would leave food out for me near the garbage bins, knowing that I was desperate, sometimes even hiding money in the food, not letting my father know that she was doing this for me. But ultimately, the responsibility to pass or fail was solely in my hands.

I had no other option but success. I would sit in the library for hours looking at the other students, knowing that they were also trying to survive.

I watched people fail and drop out, and while I was fluctuating between being on and off probation, I hung in there and worked hard. In my second to last semester, I received two Bs and two Cs and was finally taken off probation. It was the first time since I had started law school that I felt confident in my ability to be successful. I went home for a two-week vacation, looking forward to registering for my last semester.

But it didn't quite work out that way.

When I returned to school, I lined up to register with everyone else but was called out by the assistant dean who was in the registrar's office. She looked at me and said, "Why are you here?"

I looked at her quizzically and responded with what I thought was obvious, "I'm here to register for my classes."

"Oh, no," she said, "You can't register. You failed your classes last semester."

"No," I said, "I passed all of them. I was even removed from probation."

But she was adamant.

It turned out that the school changed the grading policy after my grades had been posted. During my two-week vacation, my two Cs suddenly became two Ds and I had been thrown out of school.

I stood in shock for a few minutes but then decided I was not going to allow all my hard work to be destroyed. I needed to find the professor who had given me the Cs.

I knew this professor well: Professor Herbert Kuvin. He was famous for yelling and berating a student for no reason simply to make his point heard. He would yell at a student for not listening and the poor student, caught off guard, would ask what he did to deserve the abuse. But that would make the professor yell even more and create a scene. Finally, he would stop yelling, compose himself, and say to the students, "That, ladies and gentlemen, is what we call righteous indignation." Usually, it would get him applause and some laughs. His classes were some of the most interesting ones in the university. My only hope was with him and with some of my own "righteous indignation."

I found him easily enough and started explaining the situation. I told him how I had worked night and day to pay for school and how my life was ruined with that changed grade.

The more I spoke, the angrier I became.

"I gave up a job! I gave up my life!

I owe money everywhere! I moved out of my home and have nowhere to go! I worked for those grades and you just changed them out of hand. You need to change them back." Professor Kuvin was silent. "You always said to stand up and fight!" I continued. "Even if the judge disagrees, you still fight. Well, here I am. I am fighting. And you need to help."

I don't know whether it was my outrage or his personal feelings against the dean, but he listened to me and brought me to the assistant dean's office demanding that I be allowed to register.

"Put him back in school, or I am personally changing his grades back," he said. When the assistant dean started to protest, he dismissed her with a wave of his hand.

Shockingly, they let me register. I had four classes to take before I could graduate, and my professor advised me to take two of them with him and the third class with a former dean recommended by Professor Kuvin. After what he did to help me, I didn't need convincing. I registered for the three classes plus an extra class on ethics and writing.

I worked hard and focused on graduation, but at the very end of the semester, with only my final exams standing between me and my diploma, I was faced with a new challenge.

Both of Professor Kuvin's exams were scheduled on Saturdays.

On the Sabbath.

I couldn't take exams on the Sabbath. I had a good relationship with him though, and I thought I'd be able to explain the situation without a problem.

He would not hear any of it.

"Not you again, Ciment! There's always a problem with you." I didn't know what to say. I tried to explain to him about the Sabbath, about why I couldn't take the exam, but he was not interested in anything I had to say.

"You are taking them on Saturday," he said, dismissing me. "There is no special time for you."

I wasn't sure what to do. I was at the end of the road, I survived school, I battled for my grades, and now, in the eleventh hour, I was not going to graduate because of the Sabbath. It was unfathomable. In desperation, I went to the two largest synagogues in Miami Beach and asked the Rabbis to write letters explaining how I could not take the exams on the Sabbath. I had hoped that their words might have more of an impact than my own. I brought the letters to Professor Kuvin, but he did not respond the way I had hoped. He was furious.

I wasn't sure how this would play out, but with the letters in his hand and with an angry grimace, he told me to come to his home on Key Biscayne at 9:00 a.m. on Sunday morning to take the tests.

That Sunday, I showed up in his driveway at 8:30 a.m. I was terrified. My hands were clammy and my heart was racing. I knew how angry the professor was at giving me the exams on an alternate day and I wasn't sure what I was walking into. I had studied harder than I ever had before and braced myself for whatever would greet me on the other side of the professor's front door.

I took a deep breath and knocked.

"Why are you so early?" he asked me after opening it.

"I wanted to make sure I had no problems. If I got a flat or if something else happened. I didn't want to be late," I explained.

He brought me into his home and told me that the exams I was going to take were different from the ones the class took. He gave me the first exam and told me I had two hours to complete it. I can't explain the absolute terror that engulfed me as I went to sit down. So much depended on this exam. I had seen students drop out and for some reason, I was still hanging on. But I knew that rope was tenuous. I knew that everything relied on these tests – my life, quite literally, was in jeopardy.

I started the exam, and I looked around Professor Kuvin's den. It was a prestigious-looking room, but one item caught my eye. On the mantel was a framed picture of a religious Jew. The man in the picture had a full beard, was dressed like a Hassid, and seemed to be praying. It was a picture that didn't fit with the rest of the decor. My professor saw me looking at the picture but told me to concentrate on the exam.

I finished the first test and took a small break. The second exam followed the same rules. Two hours. Different exam than the class. I worked for the entire two hours.

I went to hand in the exam and he asked me how I did. To be honest, I wasn't sure. They were difficult exams and I struggled through them. But I gave them everything I had, and I told him that.

"I took everything you taught me and put all I knew from your teaching into the exam. I put my entire being into the answers and the test."

He looked at me in silence for a moment and then pointed to the picture I had noticed.

"I saw you looking at my grandfather," he said. He must have seen the look of shock on my face. "You know I am Catholic," he continued, "but my grandfather was a fine, Jewish religious man. Perhaps one of the finest I've known."

I stood there stunned.

With that, he took those two tests I handed him, the tests that I worked for hours on, the tests that my graduation hinged upon, and wrote an A on each of them. He didn't even open them to see what I had written. I tried to thank him, but he simply put his hands on my shoulders and said, "Good luck, Ciment."

In my last semester of law school, taking two difficult exams from one of the toughest professors in the school, I scored a top grade.

The other teacher, the former dean, whose class Professor Kuvin had recommended I take, asked me to frame about 60 pictures for his den. I framed them all and even hung them up for him. When he asked for a bill, I refused to give him one. I scored a top grade from him as well.

The dean who originally pushed the grade changes was eventually fired but not until many students had dropped out or been forced to leave. Only 27 out of the original class of 173 graduated. I was the only one on probation.

I'd like to say I graduated because I was so smart, but I knew the truth and saw it in Professor Kuvin's eyes that day I took his exam in his den. I graduated because I put the Sabbath first and probably reminded him of an ancestor long ago whom he respected and loved, and who would also not have taken an exam on the Sabbath.

THERE ARE NO COINCIDENCES IN EUROPE

*A*FTER FINALLY FINISHING LAW SCHOOL AND TAKING the bar exam, I went on a trip to Europe with my friend Warren. We bought *Frommer's Europe on $5 a Day* on traveling without spending so much money. After years of law school and working so hard, a trip to Europe was well-earned. Additionally, though my father had sold his business, he pivoted his work and focused solely on buying and selling instead of manufacturing. He moved to a small store on Fifth Street in Miami Beach to run his business.

But traveling through Europe wasn't just a joyride for me and Warren.

As a kid, I always worked in my father's picture frame business in New York. Every year, a man by the name of Sam Brodst would come to Florida with his paintings to sell. He was the owner of the Vienna Art Publishing Company and had the exclusive on paintings that my father would buy for his company. Every painting we bought for the business came from Sam Brodst. My father was always looking for another supplier but was never able to find anyone else who carried the original paintings that Brodst provided for us.

It always bothered me.

Brodst was a conceited man. Each year when he came to Florida, my father would take him out to dinner and show him around. He was the only man with the paintings we needed, and he knew it. It aggravated me to no end.

When I went to Europe on this trip, I decided to find the source of those paintings and the elaborate frames that went along with them.

We landed in Paris and I began my search. I went to 20 galleries, I called people but no one knew about the paintings. I knew those paintings that Brodst sold my father had to be coming from Europe and I wanted to find them. I searched everywhere. As we traveled through Europe, I continued to search for the paintings. I searched in Belgium, Germany, Paris, and Madrid. No matter where I went, no one could help me. I even interviewed taxi drivers in the hopes that they could give me some kind of information. All to no avail. Eventually, I wound up in Naples and went to the local American Express office to pick up my mail.

I had told my father that my travels would take me to Naples and that he should send me a letter with my bar exam results. Sure enough, when I presented my ID, a letter was there waiting for me.

I failed the bar.

I stared at the letter, speechless. My heart sank. I could not believe the terrible news. I was devastated and heartbroken. I had worked for almost five years with the expectation of becoming a lawyer, and suddenly, with one succinct notice in a mailbox in Naples, my future was destroyed. More importantly, I could not imagine going back to the United States with this knowledge. I was consumed by shame and desperation. I didn't know what to do.

I went back to the hostel where I was staying, and another option opened up to me. Another person at the hostel gave me the idea to go to Israel.

At the time, the Eichmann trial was taking place in Israel, and there was a special offer of $75 to travel round trip to Israel for ten days. Seven hundred Romanian refugees were traveling on the boat, and I had a chance to join them.

Seventy-five dollars was a lot of money. I was living on $5 a day and that included room and board. But my new friend said the magic words that sold me on taking the trip. He said he could show me how to make a lot of money and earn back the money for the trip. Having just failed the bar, the possibility of earning money was appealing.

I asked him how that was possible, and he gave me the following idea.

"You're going to buy Ban-Lon polo shirts for $3, and you'll sell them for $10. And you'll buy portable radios for $8, and you can sell them for $40." He was telling me to get into the black market in Israel.

I trusted him. And more importantly, I trusted the possibilities that awaited me across the sea. With the news of my failed exam, the idea of traveling and possibly becoming successful outside the United States was rather appealing. So Warren and I purchased the shirts and the radios and set off on the two-day journey to Israel.

When we arrived in Israel, we found a cheap place to stay. It was $3 a night for a suite with a terrace looking over the Mediterranean Sea. The proprietors were a woman who had numbers on her arm and her 14-year-old child. She had a husband, but he was very sick.

There was something about this woman that touched me. I liked her. She also gravitated to me. Her daughter was obsessed with the portable radios that I was carrying but didn't have the $40 to purchase it. I decided to make her an offer. We were going to be staying at the hotel for ten days. I asked her to let us stay there in exchange for the radio, and then she could sell it on her own if she wanted.

She agreed. But she also offered me a piece of advice. She told me that she could tell me how to make money in Israel. She took me to *Lilienblum* Street the next day where people were trading money. It was my first introduction to the Israeli black market exchange. As my interpreter, she spoke for me. I was able to exchange money at a high rate, and I went to hotels asking customers to exchange money with me instead of the hotels. At the end of my ten days in Israel, I had earned a few hundred dollars. In 1962, that was a great deal of money.

I begged Warren to stay with me in Israel instead of going back to the States. I was making a lot of money and thought it made sense to stay. I also felt that I had no options in America, with that failure notification weighing heavily on me. I pleaded with him. If he would stay with me, then I could continue earning money and forget about practicing law. But Warren had been accepted to medical school and needed to return, and I didn't want to leave my friend. So we returned to Naples, but this time with considerably more money in our pockets. Instead of staying at a youth hostel, we decided to stay at a nice hotel.

Warren wanted to take a cab to the hotel, which made sense. I tried to convince him to walk. We had been on a boat for two days and I felt that it would do us good to stretch our legs and move. It was a long walk, but for some reason, he agreed with me.

Twenty minutes into that walk, I came across a store. In the window of the store were the paintings that I had been searching for since the start of my trip. Right there, sitting in front of me. I hadn't even been looking for them; they just appeared.

I couldn't believe it. My heart stopped. To say I was shocked would be an understatement.

Apparently, there was a school in Naples filled with students who painted the pictures daily. They completed around 100 paintings a day – basically just commercial art – but they were the paintings my father bought. This one store in Naples that I stumbled upon on my walk with my friend was the source for the Vienna Art Publishing Company. They actually owned the art school where the paintings were created. I felt like I had struck gold. The price was almost half of what my father paid to Mr. Brost.

I thought back to that moment when I was nine years old and earned my first 12 cents shining shoes. At that time, I felt like I was a millionaire. And now, as an adult, and through a series of inexplicable events – choosing to walk instead of taking a taxi – I had the key to earning a fortune. Between the paintings I discovered and the money I could make in Israel, I was looking at returning to the United States with a bright future. Warren lent me $2,000 that day so I could purchase all the paintings and bring them back to the United States.

I could have become the largest distributor in the United States. Even more shocking was what happened next. The next part of our trip took us to Amsterdam. Warren wanted to continue on to Copenhagen, but I had met a girl in Amsterdam I liked. I didn't want to separate from Warren, but he knew I liked this girl and so he said, "Look, you stay here. I'll be back in two days. It's only two days."

It was unbelievable that he was willing to continue without me and that he would leave me behind on the trip that we had planned. I felt bad about that. However, staying behind opened up yet another avenue for me in the business world.

The girl, as it turned out, was an art student who connected me to one of the largest frame factories that did not have an American contract. Between the frames in Amsterdam and the paintings in Naples, I was looking at creating the largest monopoly in America. Also, for the first time since hearing the news of failing the bar, I felt like I could return home. I had prospects and I could make money.

When I returned to the States, I didn't want to tell my father what I had discovered overseas. So I hired an old friend, Murray Rubin, to take the samples I brought back and sell them to my father. I even printed up a phony business card.

My father was ecstatic. He bought all the samples and placed an order with Murray for $10,000. That's almost $75,000 in today's terms.

That night I came home, and my father was surrounded by the samples – my samples – and he was beaming.

"Look what I purchased!" he said. "Murray Rubin represents this company called Creations Unlimited from Sarasota, Florida. Look at the paintings!" My father was beside himself with joy. I didn't tell him that it was me until later that night. I was sitting at the dinner table with my parents and posed this question to my mother.

"Ma," I started, "my friend came to me with a problem. He is afraid to tell his father something because his father would be embarrassed. He doesn't know what to do. He asked me for advice. Should he tell his father the truth? Or should he lie to his father?"

They both agreed that the friend should tell the father. "The father will forgive his son for lying," my father said. "He should tell the truth."

I got up from the table, walked out of the room, and then came back. I looked at my father and told him the truth. That Murray Rubin didn't sell anything from Sarasota. He was my representative.

"I'm Sarasota," I told him. "Everything I said I could do, I did. I now have the largest connection from the European factories to sell in America. We could be the biggest company in America. I have all the sources."

He was completely shocked. But I went on.

"Pop," I said, "I'm giving it all to you. I want to pass the bar. I want to practice law. All I want to do is sell for you so that I can support myself while I build my business. But all this is for you."

Something had changed when I returned. Since getting the letter about failing the bar, I dropped all my dreams of practicing law. In a panic, I decided to just find jobs that would allow me to make money and move on. But when I arrived in the United States, I thought about the years I put in. I had sweated and worked harder than I ever had to maintain my grades and pass my classes. I sacrificed five years of my life. While the despair upon learning I had failed was raw and real, I decided to not walk away. I was going to give the bar a second shot.

The decision to retake the bar still puzzles me today. I had a huge opportunity but something compelled me to lean toward law again. Practically, I knew that the frame business would always be there for me. In that sense, I really had nothing to lose. But retaking the bar and pursuing law, even after I had a stable future in the framing business, was a decision that ran counter to everything that had motivated me previously.

I reached out to a friend of mine named George Nachwalter. He was a smart guy and had passed the bar on the first attempt. I called him up and asked him for advice. He gave me the key to unlocking the exam.

"For each question," he explained, "find the five Ws: Who, What, Where, When, and Why. That's the key to every question."

It was like he had given me an amulet for understanding. His simple advice changed the way I approached the exam. It broke down the questions clearly. In fact, those five Ws are the questions needed to approach every lawsuit.

Three months later I retook the bar and passed.

Finding those paintings in Naples changed my life completely. It allowed me to have money in my pocket, and it supported me as I built my practice. The circumstances of finding them was nothing short of a miracle. Looking at the events that led me to walking into the center of Naples that day and happening upon the very paintings I needed, choosing to stay with a woman who would connect me to the very picture frames I needed – it is all remarkable. Something else was at play in those decisions.

To this day, I am unable to comprehend or explain how all the pieces fell into place – how I searched throughout Europe for paintings that I later stumbled upon on a random walk through Naples. In fact, even my decision to retry the bar exam was astonishing because I had been so sure I was going to give up law.

Looking back at it now, I feel that there was something other worldly guiding me in the direction I needed to go.

SEEING THE SETUP IN THE SETBACK

---

*L*ANDING THAT FIRST OFFICIAL JOB AFTER LAW SCHOOL is a pivotal moment in life. It represents everything you have worked for, all your dreams for the future. It is supposed to be the launching pad for your career. For me, after finally passing the bar, getting my first law job was going to be the setup for the rest of my life. More than that, because I had struggled through school and graduated law school by the skin of my teeth, landing an official job as a lawyer was, in my mind, a moment of ultimate triumph.

As usual, things did not initially pan out quite the way I had hoped.

My father's framing business was doing well, especially with the connections I had made for him, and even though I was earning money on my own just selling paintings, I knew it was time to start working in the field I really wanted. That job, a job at the city attorney's office, was offered to me by a man named Joe Wanick.

Joe Wanick had promised me the job and I was raring to go. It was a perfect place for a newly minted lawyer to start. Originally, I was supposed to start work in September, but I soon realized that September was filled with the High Holidays. Between Rosh Hashanah, Yom Kippur, and Sukkot, I was going to need to take many days off. I didn't think it would be a good idea to start my career with so many missed work days, so I asked if we could move my employment start date to October 1.

To my relief, he agreed.

Getting a job with the city attorney was a powerful moment. I was incredibly proud of where I was going and I did not keep that to myself. I told my friends, my family, and everyone who knew me. My entire synagogue knew that I was starting a job with the city attorney. I spent that month of September filled with pride and anticipation.

On October 1, I showed up to work, briefcase in hand, freshly pressed suit, ready to start.

And then, the unthinkable happened.

"I'm sorry. You don't work here. Your office was taken by another attorney." I stood in front of the secretary and couldn't believe what she had said. The color drained from my face. To say I was shocked was an understatement.

"What do you mean?" I asked.

"Mr. Wanick hired someone else while you were out," she replied nonchalantly.

I stood there dumbfounded. Shame crept into the corners of my face. How could this have happened? And then, I thought back to the previous month, to my prideful boasting. How could I return to my family and all my friends and tell them I didn't have a job? Worse, how would I find a new job? My shame and shock quickly gave way to anger. This was unfair. It was unthinkable. I knew I needed to do something.

Ignoring the protests of the secretary, I walked down the hall to Wanick's office, barged in, yelling and screaming at the absolute betrayal. I was promised a job. How could he have done this to me?

But my ranting and raving made no difference. All Wanick did was usher me out of the building, tell me to be quiet and that he was sorry, but the job was given to someone else.

There was nothing I could do.

I left the building. I was numb. My career was ending before it even got started. The hatred for Wanick swelled within me. He destroyed my hopes and ambitions and left me crushed.

I wasn't sure what to do, so I went to my friend Bob Grover. He didn't have much advice for me and understood my predicament, but said that maybe I should set up an interview where he was working, with an attorney named Jay Swidler. When I was graduating law school, I had almost had a job with Swidler, but it never panned out as I had left for a trip to Europe and failed the bar. I knew it was unlikely a job was still available, but I had since passed the bar and Bob convinced me to go in for an interview anyway. I really had nothing to lose, so I set it up.

In truth, it wasn't really an interview. It was more like a lunch date. A chance to talk to Swidler. Jay Swidler was a stand-up guy. He met with me and interviewed me, but also told me that there was neither a job available nor a free office even if he wanted to hire me. I didn't know what I was going to do, but an idea suddenly emerged as he was gently telling me I had no job.

"Jay," I said, "please accept what I'm going to say to you with an open mind." Swidler looked at me quizzically, not sure what I was going to say. I went on. "I want to work only for you. For your firm. I don't want to wait around for an opening. I want to work immediately. I know you don't need anybody and so that's why I'm going to make you an offer.

"I know you don't have an office available for me, but I walked through your offices before we met and I saw that you have a filing room. All I need is a small folding table, like a card table, and a chair. I'll buy both of those and set up shop in that filing room. I'll work 80 hours a week. I want to go to your hearings, your trials, your meetings. I want to do your gofer work and then I'll come in every morning at seven thirty and I'll work until eleven at night in between."

I don't know where I got the nerve to say that.

I don't even know how that idea came into my head. It was a crazy proposition, but I was so desperate for work, so desperate to come home with pride instead of the shame that hounded me since losing the job at the city attorney's office.

Shockingly, I could see that Swidler was contemplating what I was saying. I didn't want to lose my moment so I threw in the proverbial icing on the cake.

"I'll work those 80 hours," I said, "and I'll pay *you* $15 a week to do it. That's how much I want this job."

Swidler looked at me and said, "Are you crazy? Are you sick? What kind of a crazy proposal is that?"

I said, "I don't need your money. I make a lot of money. But I want to work for you." I couldn't decide if Swidler thought I was crazy or if he was taking me seriously. I wasn't sure if he was going to take my offer or throw me out of the building. It seemed like forever until he finally spoke.

"I'll buy you the chair," he finally said. "I'll buy you the table and I'll put a phone in that room. And I accept your offer of working 80 hours a week, but I'm going to pay *you* the $15 a week."

I took the job.

My salary was actually $14.03 because he needed to take off 97 cents for taxes, but I didn't care. Three months after that conversation, he raised my salary to $50 a week. Three months after that he raised it again to $75. Three months later my salary went to $100 a week and then eventually to $125. At that point, Bobby and I decided we wanted to be junior partners. I had only been working there for one year when I approached Swidler about becoming a partner. Swidler didn't laugh at me or berate me. Instead, he said, "I really don't need any partners, but I also don't want you guys to leave me. I want to help you start your firm."

Now it was my turn to be shocked.

"Stay here in my office," he continued. "I'll give you one of my secretaries, you'll pay half of her salary and she will do your work, and I'll give you 25 small cases to try." In addition, he gave us two offices to lease in the building.

It was a kind and benevolent gesture that allowed me and Bobby to work for the next few years and build our practice up. It was a job that created the foundation for my law practice and even though the circumstances of getting the job were far from standard, looking back, it seems as if all the pieces needed to fall together that way. I think about how upset I was in Joe Wanick's office that day he told me I didn't have the job I was expecting. Now, I thank God that he did that. If I had worked for him, I would have hated it – I did not like the city's attorney office - and in all likelihood I would have gone back to my father and worked for him. This one moment in time made all the other moments happen. I realized that I was pushed out of that position to find Jay Swidler and eventually go into my own practice.

I certainly don't think it's a stretch to say that many times in my life, what appeared to be a setback, was actually a setup for something far greater. This was certainly one of those times.

THE LAW OFFICES OF GROVER & CIMENT

*T*HE BIRTH OF GROVER & CIMENT IS INTERESTING BEYOND the humble beginnings in Swidler's office. Bobby and I had bought a townhouse and we were living together when we decided to go into partnership. The first question we had was what we would call the firm.

I asked him, "What are you thinking? What should it be called?"

"Well," he says, "if you want to use age, I'm eight months older than you so that would qualify for my name to be first: Grover & Ciment."

"I don't think that's a good measure for deciding on the name, "I said.

"Okay," he continued, "Why don't we take a deck of cards and we'll shuffle it up and cut the deck? Whoever gets the high hand, he'll be the first name."

I said, "No, I don't like that idea either." I realized he wanted his name first. "I'll tell you what, Bobby, I don't want to cut the deck. I don't want to play cards. I don't want to gamble. I want the firm to be Grover & Ciment. For nothing. I'm giving it to you. All I want to do is make money. I'm not egotistical, I don't need my name up front. That's it. It's Grover-Ciment. You got it." I figured that I owed him that. That and much more.

That was the beginning.

In November of 1963, we had been working for close to a year when Bob said to me, "You know, you're pretty well known in the Jewish community, your father has a successful framing business, why don't you run for a city office?" It was the first time I had thought of running for public office, but it wasn't something I thought was a good idea. The main idea was to network and hand out business cards and get some new clients, not really to actually win an election.

"You're not going to win," Bob explained, "But the publicity will be good. We'll invest money into it and we'll hand out cards with the firm's name, and we'll get clients that way."

When he put it that way, I agreed. It was a good idea. So I went down to city hall to pick up the application to run. Later that day, I received a call from Joe Malek.

Joe Malek was a prominent real estate attorney. He had just run for attorney general of Florida, and lost. He was also a cantor and he was popular with the senior citizens. He represented hundreds of them. I didn't know him at all, but there he was on my phone, wanting to speak to me.

"Hi, my name is Joe Malek, and I hear you want to run for city commission." I was on my guard a bit. After all, I didn't know why he would be calling me. "I'd like to meet with you to talk to you about it," he continued, "because I'm running also."

I was a bit intrigued. I wasn't sure what he wanted. So I asked him, "When do you want to meet?"

He said, "Well, I understand you are a Sabbath observer and you daven at Rabbi Rackovsky's shul. I'll come down there on the Sabbath, and we'll talk then."

Sure enough, on the Sabbath day, Joe Malek was at the shul's kiddush, and we talked. I explained to him that I was only running to drum up publicity for my new law firm and that the commissioner race would allow me to meet many people, potentially get new clients, and get my name out there.

Malek listened and made me an offer.

"I understand what you want to do," he said. "So how about instead of running, you become my campaign manager? You can hand out as many business cards as you want, and I'll help you build your practice."

It was an interesting offer. It would give me the opportunity to learn firsthand about city politics, it would give me some measure of prominence, and if he lost, it was no sweat off my back. I could be involved in a campaign without having to worry about losing. I agreed. I became his campaign manager.

He lost by 113 votes. Even though he lost, I was showered with compliments on the campaign telling me what a fantastic job I did. For me, it didn't really make that much of a difference because my purpose was about building my practice. Over the course of the campaign, I handed out hundreds of cards and leaflets and got new clients.

A few years later in 1965, Joe Malek decided to run again. He came to me and asked if I would be his campaign manager. I had found many new clients the last time, and so it seemed like a good decision to help him out again. But I also started thinking about my own political future.

"Joe," I said, "I'll help you. I'll be your campaign manager. But you have to promise me that if I ever run, you will back me no matter what."

"No question," he answered. "Win or lose, I will back you."

So began my second foray into political campaigning. But this time, the results were better. Joe Malek won the commission seat by over 2,000 votes. It was a great moment, but again, I had helped him mainly to help myself and my fledgling law firm. After the win, I went back to my practice, focusing on the new clients I acquired during the campaign.

In the background of all this, I also was focusing on my personal life. As my career was taking off, I realized it was time to also settle down and start a family. I wasn't in college anymore; I was an established man with a promising career.

LOVE AND FATE

---

*T*HE TALMUD SAYS THAT GETTING TWO PEOPLE TOGETHER in marriage is sometimes as difficult as splitting the sea.

Choosing a spouse is a decision that I never took lightly, but even that decision was guided by destiny. At the time, it didn't seem that way, but like everything else in my life, it took some time and distance to see the guidance that was leading me to find my true match. It wasn't a straight route.

While I was still in law school, I dated a woman named Judy and had become engaged to marry her. It would have been a good marriage for me at the time. Her family owned a large company and they offered me a job. Many of my friends who were worried about graduating from the University of Miami Law School were looking to marry into families who could support them. It wasn't a completely crazy idea. With so many students failing out every semester, they sought some sort of security.

But I also really liked Judy. I didn't look at the relationship the same way the guys in my class did. I dated Judy, and we both decided that we would get married. I proposed and she accepted. My friends were excited for me, my parents were happy. Her family planned a lavish engagement party for us.

Four days prior to the event, her parents took me out for a drink and asked me the following.

"Judy is used to the finest things," her mother explained. "She's traveled the world. She's been to the best restaurants. The famous museums. Would you allow her to eat out while you're traveling? Judy knows how you feel about eating non-kosher. I figured it would be best if I asked you for her."

I was shocked.

I had discussed my religious convictions with Judy and told her that I would not compromise on that.

"Did Judy ask you to speak to me?" I asked.

"We knew you were a worldly person. Well-educated and well-traveled," her mother continued. "Judy wanted me to ask you. To make sure you were okay with it."

I thanked her parents for the evening and went to meet Judy.

Keeping the Sabbath saved my life in law school.

Compromising on those religious values at that point in my life, after learning firsthand how important it was, was not an option. I went out with Judy, told her how I felt, and took back the ring. I had two friends call the more than 300 people who were planning to join us for our engagement party and let them know the party, and the marriage, was canceled.

It was not an easy thing to do, by any stretch of the imagination. I was devastated in more ways than one, but it was something that I knew was so important for my life. I felt it as strongly as I did that day I told my professor that I couldn't take the exams on Saturday. My values and beliefs were strong and following them had always led me to the right decisions.

It was a few years later that I started thinking of marriage again. It was when my career was taking off and I was becoming moderately successful. I wasn't in college anymore, I was an established man with a promising career and realized it was time to get married and start a family.

When I met Joan, the woman who would eventually be my wife, our first date did not go so well. I didn't think she was going to be "the one." At the time, my partner, Bobby, and I used to throw open houses at our townhouse. We would invite guys and girls to come over for drinks and food and generally have a great time and in the process, get new clients. I invited Joan to come to one of our famous open houses, but she was out of town. Two weeks later, when she returned, she called me. She thanked me for the invitation and told me about her roommate from Boston, Carol, was staying with her and she wanted to set her up with me. I agreed and told her we would double-date, as I wanted to set Joan up with my partner, Bob. It was a great plan, but I wound up spending most of the time talking to Joan instead of Carol. As I walked her home that night, I mentioned that I had tickets to the circus and asked her if she wanted to join me.

We dated for five months before we were married.

I set down parameters from the beginning. I told her that the Sabbath and keeping kosher were not negotiable. She needed to be on the same page as me and needed to know that her life with me would be an Orthodox Jewish life.

That's the beauty of knowing you have met your "*bashert*," your soulmate. Joan Kratish became my wife, the woman I would build a family with, and the woman who would stand beside me through everything life would send our way. Most important to me, even though she did not grow up in an Orthodox home, she agreed that we would live an Orthodox Jewish life together. My experience with Judy, the pain of a broken engagement, and the humbling moment when I had to tell everyone that the wedding was off prepared me for finding the right woman. It also solidified the values that I learned from my parents and grandparents which I would not sacrifice, no matter how tempting.

Joan and I were married in a beautiful affair on July 4, 1965. It was Independence Day and the joke, of course, was that it was the last day of my independence. But the truth was, it was a turning point in my life, and like everything in my life, there wasn't a straight line to get there.

Had Joan not been out of town, she would have just been another girl at the townhouse. I wouldn't have been able to connect to her the way I was able to if she had just been one of the 75 other women that came to my open house that evening.

Every experience, every choice, every step, was influenced by a force outside of myself that made sure, regardless of the challenges, that I was on a path chosen for me.

PHOTO SECTION

With my parents in 1946. I am wearing my first suit.

Tepper and I catch a big one, 1961.

Joan and me on our wedding day, July 4, 1965.

With Jackie Gleason, 1967.

Ciment city councilman election campaign ads, 1967.

With Rabbi Sender Gross and Abba Eban in 1976.

With comic legend Milton Berle, 1978.

With my mom and brother Mel, 1979.

Running for Mayor, 1981.

Election night with my family, November 1981.

With Henry Kissinger in 1982.

With Dr. Maurice Jaffe, founder of the Great Synagogue in Jerusalem, 1982.

With Mayor Ed Koch of New York City, 1982.

With Prime Minister Jacques Chirac of France, 1982.

With Prime Minister Yitzhak Rabin in 1982.

With Marvin Hier (left) and Simon Wiesenthal (center), 1983.

With comedian Jackie Mason in 1983.

With Ariel Sharon, 1997.

Joan and me with Prime Minister Benjamin Netanyahu in 1999.

My wonderful family, 2021.

POLITICAL ASPIRATIONS

*I*N 1967, I WAS AT A BOXING MATCH WITH MY FRIENDS Paul Glassman and Bobby Goodman. At the arena, there were many people campaigning for various political positions. State representative, commissioner – all kinds of positions. It was a Floyd Patterson championship fight, and so the arena was packed.

Paul Glassman looked at all the candidates running around the arena and remarked on how young they were.

"Look at these little pipsqueaks running for office," he said. "Norman, why don't you run for commissioner?"

The irony of his statement was that he didn't know I had worked as a campaign manager for two elections. And they also didn't know that I had been thinking of running for the past four years and was going to try to run for a commissioner seat.

I didn't tell them that, though. I simply feigned interest and said that it was a good idea and that I would think about it.

"If you run," Paul said, "I'll give you the first $1,000 for the campaign." That would amount to roughly $10,000 today.

Three days later there was a knock at my door. It was a Saturday afternoon. I opened the door to see Bobby Goodman.

"I knew you wouldn't answer the phone today, so I came over instead," he said. He walked into my home carrying a package filled with items for a campaign – a campaign for Norman Ciment. He had bumper stickers and signs that said "Elect Ciment" and "Rebuild Miami Beach with Ciment." I couldn't believe it. Why would he have created all this?

He told me that he wanted to be my campaign manager and that he wanted me to run.

"I can't afford you," I said.

"I know," he answered, "but I also know you're a straight guy. I want to do this for you, and I know you will pay me back whenever you can pay me back. I trust you."

My firm was growing at this point. We had two new junior partners with us, and Bobby Grover agreed that I should take Goodman's offer and run for commissioner.

The day I was going to file for my candidacy, I talked to Joe Malek and let him know that I was planning on running against the incumbent, Bernie Frank. The incumbent's father was president of the largest senior citizens organization in Miami Beach, and he was friendly with the other 15 presidents of different senior groups. In short, he was an incredibly powerful and well-connected man. His win was practically a given.

When I told Malek that I was planning on running, he turned pale. Most of his constituents were loyal to the incumbent. There was no way Malek would back me. It wasn't worth it to him because he was sure I would not win.

It was a sharp betrayal of an understanding we had made and of our supposed friendship. I couldn't believe it. I had worked for him through two campaigns and he had given his word that should I ever run for office, he would back me. And there I was, finally calling in the commitment to back me, and he turned me down.

I was seething with anger.

"Let me tell you something," I said, "if you don't keep your word, your reputation will be destroyed. I will personally ruin you. You won't be able to get elected dog catcher in the city when I am finished with you. I'll let everyone know that you aren't true to your word."

But he would not back down. He would not back me.

In some ways, this propelled me on.

Grover and I opened up our campaign headquarters and started working. Goodman, my campaign manager, was working for free, and I was committed to running in the race.

The deadline to file for candidacy was 5:00 p.m. on a Saturday. I had filed early but starting at 3:00 p.m. on Saturday, my phone started ringing off the hook. It rang all afternoon, but since it was the Sabbath, I did not pick it up. When I was finally able to answer, I heard the news that Milton Gaynor, the vice president of the largest bank in Miami Beach, had filed to run as well. He also had two partners, one of whom was Arthur Courshon, the former national financial chairman of the National Democratic Party. The other partner was U.S. Senator Claude Pepper.

I was suddenly facing a formidable race, not just against the incumbent. It was a challenging situation and I could not win. But I had made the commitment and could not back down.

To gain name recognition and support, we invested a significant amount of money in car toppers, posters, bumper stickers, and campaign handouts. The idea was to plaster the city with my name and image so that people would recognize me when I spoke at various clubs, condo buildings, and meetings. We worked hard on crafting my first speech, refining it multiple times over a week.

However, my initial appearance at a major hotel in front of 400 people was a disaster. The audience looked disappointed, and I realized that my formal, rehearsed speech wasn't working. I decided to be more authentic and speak the way I normally did, as I wasn't a polished orator but more of a rabble-rouser. I threw away the speech that had been rewritten four times and spoke extemporaneously. I ad-libbed. The subsequent speeches improved, but my real challenge arose when I discovered there were three races happening concurrently, including the mayoral race.

During this campaign, I faced multiple hurdles. Most clubs endorsed the incumbent, my main opponent, and he orchestrated limiting my speaking time. Despite the odds, my campaign gained unexpected momentum when friends, customers from my dad's business, and fellow community members rallied to support me. We started distributing brochures door-to-door, and I gained the reputation of being a fighter for fairness and free choice.

As the campaign progressed, I continued to engage with the community, and my partners offered legal assistance and other services to those in need. When the incumbent saw our growing popularity, he came to make a deal with me. Desperate for financial support, we considered dropping out of the race, even requesting

$8,000 from the incumbent to reimburse our expenses, but he declined. However, we did strike a formal deal. Since we were both running opposite a serious contender, it was possible there would be a runoff. We agreed that if he came in second, I would endorse him, and if I came in second, he would endorse me. We shook hands and repeated the deal. I didn't think I had a chance against the incumbent and certainly felt I had no chance against this powerhouse banker.

Throughout the campaign, we overcame challenges, built connections, and earned respect from the community. The experience taught me the value of authenticity, determination, and connecting with people on a personal level, and our campaign started to gain some momentum. Joe Malek eventually walked into my office. He was apologetic and contrite and said that he changed his mind. He brought his entire family to help out in the campaign – his wife, his mother-in-law – everyone was working for my campaign. Unbelievable!

Joe Malek, now the vice mayor, used his connections to secure the Deauville Hotel for a Sunday rally. He also managed to get two restaurants to donate food for a free brunch, to which we invited all the senior clubs, even though they were expected to support Bernard Frank, the incumbent.

To our surprise, about 500 people showed up, and the reception was fantastic. While they mainly came because it was a free social event, we noticed a shift in people's attitudes toward us. Recognizing the importance of a clear platform, we worked on crafting specific messages that resonated with voters. Initially, I hadn't expected to win. I was merely seeking to start building my law practice. But circumstances were changing.

In 1963, Joe Malek lost by a narrow margin of 113 votes, but in

1965, he triumphed over the same opponent by 2,000 votes. When I ran in 1967, I faced formidable opponents, including the influential banker Milton Gaynor, backed by U.S. Senator Claude Pepper and Arthur Courshon, the former national financial chairman. I secmed insignificant in comparison, with little money, no background, and only four years of legal practice.

I refused to give up.

Despite the challenges, we continued because of the dedication of our friends and volunteers. I couldn't back down. The city was divided, with various organizations endorsing our opponents. To counter this, I adopted an attacking strategy, highlighting the negative aspects of the bankers and incumbents while promising change and protection for citizens.

My campaign targeted the 60 percent of people who had never voted before. I visited every single apartment, speaking to each resident and leaving campaign literature in the form of door hangers for them to distribute in their buildings. To counter the time constraints at the speeches, I finally stepped up. As they were shutting me down during one speech, something came over me. I grabbed the microphone and started yelling in Yiddish to the people who had gathered to hear the candidates.

"Why won't they let me speak?" I yelled. "What are they afraid of?" The crowd quieted and one woman responded in Yiddish: "Let the kid talk!" Soon the entire room was chanting along with her. This turned the voters around. I urged people not to listen to their organization's leaders but to vote for the candidate they believed would bring positive change.

Despite the lack of media coverage, our persistence and increasing support at rallies caught the attention of Larry King, then a cub reporter in Miami, who started writing about the underdog candidate gaining ground. Surprisingly, some people began secretly donating to our campaign to protect their interests in case I won, further fueling our belief that things were changing in our favor.

In our campaign, we followed the philosophy of Ho Chi Minh when he fought against France, comparing ourselves to ants taking on an elephant. We targeted the non-voters and broke up the senior organizations, persuading about 25 percent of them to vote for us by establishing personal connections, and offering money and jobs so that key people would be working for me.

It was a war for each vote, and we engaged in campaign car parades, marches, and other tireless efforts to get our message across. Despite starting as an unknown kid with no money, no backing, and no support from established groups, we challenged the entire power structure of the candidates, hoping to force a runoff election. This was an explosive turn of events, and the city was now witnessing a David vs. Goliath battle for the election.

The vote for the commissioner race was set in the week of the Six Day War in Israel, a time of tension and conflict. Larry King noted that the incumbent candidate remained the favorite, with the banker closely behind, but he saw a possibility that I, Norman Ciment, might surge ahead to victory.

Our campaign faced an uphill battle as every civic group endorsed Milton Gaynor, the banker, or Bernard Frank, the incumbent, leaving us without any endorsements. However, a chance meeting with the president of the chartered Democratic Club from years back brought a glimmer of hope. He agreed to sign a letter of endorsement, even though the club's membership had dwindled over the years. We printed this endorsement as a full-page ad on the eve of the election. Even though there were only 150 members of the club, the ad stated that there were 7,000 members. The president effectively shut down any claims of fraud by explaining that there had been 7,000 members of the organization "for all time." We sent out a letter from Marvin Weinstein the day before the election. Marvin Weinstein was my partner, but he shared the same last name as the vice mayor, Lenny Weinstein. Our ad smudged the first name so only a discerning reader could see that it wasn't the vice mayor making the endorsement! They went crazy!

Creating a campaign that targeted people who didn't vote was our key weapon in winning. Additionally, we hired friends who agreed to drive 500 people to the polls who would not otherwise have had access. Joan Ciment became the greatest campaigner of our entire group. She could walk into a group of 75 or more people, not knowing anyone, and in minutes she was able to capture their attention. The first time that happened, we left her at Morton Towers, a building of 1,500 apartments. We told her to solicit all the people at the pool. She panicked. Three hours later, when we picked her up, she was positively ebullient. She explained how friendly everyone was, and how my brochure with two pictures – one of me with Jackie Gleason and the other of Joan with our son Ivan – was warmly received. She said the whole building gave her a great reception. The campaigner in her was born that day!

Between the absentee voters and the new voters, and through persistence and connecting with people, we came in first and forced a runoff election. The city was stunned and we were in shock. I came in first and Bernie Frank, the incumbent, came in third. So it came down to a battle between me and Milton Gaynor, the banker.

Frank, who had promised to back me, broke his word. He endorsed the banker. However, his father, who was the president of one of the largest senior organizations, came to visit me and said, "I am ashamed of my son who broke his word, but I am here with my entire organization to keep my word and support you. We will help you get elected."

My opponent brought in Senator Claude Pepper, who was loved by all the senior citizens because he was their representative in Congress. He campaigned in the streets of Miami Beach. They took out huge ads in newspapers and on television and distributed thousands of leaflets throughout the city. It was a huge fight, a major battle for every vote.

However, we gathered tremendous momentum with the senior organizations that controlled South Beach. And in the end, despite the betrayal from the incumbent and the power of the banker, I won.

In my new role, the first major decision was whether to fire Joe Wanick, the city attorney who had previously denied me a job opportunity.

Joe came into my office and literally got on his knees and begged me for his job. He confessed that he saw me as a potential threat to his job and that was why he didn't hire me before. I had conflicting emotions, wanting to retaliate for his actions. I hated him. I wanted to torture him and make him feel as helpless as I felt when I showed up for a job that I had been promised.

I don't know where the revelation came from, but I felt that I would one day need him.

Instead of destroying him, I made the decision to turn him into an ally. I struck a deal with him; I would keep him on if he swore loyalty to me, informed me of city hall matters, and guided me through the intricacies of the job. He accepted the terms, and together, we accomplished much more than I ever imagined.

One significant issue was rent control, an idea I advocated despite knowing it would negatively impact the city's residents. I secretly instructed Wanick to draft the ordinance with deliberate constitutional flaws. The council approved it and it became law, but as anticipated, it was ruled unconstitutional after two years. The senior leaders behind it had faded away, and no one knew about our strategic maneuver except for my closest confidants.

Another crucial opportunity arose when the U.S. Corps of Engineers offered us $30 million to build a 300-foot-wide beach to protect the city from erosion and potential destruction. However, the city commission voted 5–2 against it due to the fear of attracting "undesirable" people and disrupting guests at the Fontainebleau, a prominent hotel. This decision proved to be costly, as the city later spent $82 million in 1982 to construct a narrower 150-foot-wide beach, missing the earlier chance to secure federal funding.

I took my role as commissioner seriously and voted to change the city landscape for the better. I persuaded the commissioners to vote on a policy change that required having doctors on ambulances throughout the city to ensure better health care during the first crucial moments of an emergency. They also voted to require landlords to pay interest on the security deposits they collected from their tenants. I secured public places that were important for the growth of the city. In particular, there was a parking garage with 400 spaces that I allowed investors to bid on for purchase. The bid included terminology that if any changes to the structure were required during construction, the cost of those changes would have to be paid by the contractor and not the city. My "no change order" saved the city several hundreds of thousands of dollars.

Over the four years I was commissioner, my partner Bob Grover and I worked hard to build up our legal practice, taking in Sherwin Stauber and Marvin Weinstein as partners.

My relationship with Joe Malek proved beneficial. Joe Malek had an actual blood brother (with a different last name) named Gene Weiss. Soon after I won, he came to me and asked me to vote for him to become judge. I knew that Bobby Grover wanted to be a judge as well, so we made a deal. The term was two years and Weiss agreed to resign after one year, opening the seat for Bobby. When the end of the year came and it was his time to resign, I was taken for a drink at Woolworths by the commissioner I made the deal with where I was told that they were unable to honor what they promised because there was tremendous pressure from the press.

Apparently, even though I kept my part of the deal, they decided to break the deal with me and not honor their words.

That wasn't going to happen on my watch.

I immediately went to Malek and explained how they were not keeping their end of the deal. I told him, "You brought me to Weinstein, who negotiated the deal, and you need to fix this and make him honor the deal we made." He argued, explaining he can't force his own brother to resign, so we went to see his brother, who explained that since I didn't have the vote, what difference did it make if he resigned? We went back and forth and at the end of the day, this man had no integrity and wasn't interested in honoring his word.

What nobody knew, not Weiss nor even his brother Joe Malek, was that I trusted no one. Even today, at the ripe old age of 87, I have noted that there are two categories of people: those who keep their word and those who don't. Most people fall into the second category, particularly if they are not truly God-fearing, religious people.

I learned this lesson early in life when a trusted, close friend went behind my back and tried to sabotage certain relationships. I learned this when the New York importer of oil paintings lied to my father about being the sole importer of oil paintings from Europe.

And so, knowing this, I actually had prepared a backup plan in case he lived up to his reputation. He did.

One year before, when we reached the original deal, I went to a man named Jim Ruby, a campaign manager for commissioner Lee Powell, and struck up a friendship. I made secret arrangements for his commissioners to vote for me. On the day of the vote, Weinstein voted "no" along with other commissioners. The very last vote was Ruby's man, Powell. When he voted the room erupted in shock. They thought they had me, but it was the other way around. The morning headlines couldn't have said it any clearer: "Weiss Ousted!" He attacked me saying "You humiliated me! You tricked me!" My response? "Get away from me! You broke your word! You have no word! Get away from me!"

From then on, people knew I was a force to be reckoned with.

In the turbulent world of politics, I learned the importance of forging alliances and making strategic decisions that might not always align with personal beliefs.

I also lost friends.

John Forte, in particular, was a close friend who owned 800 apartments in Miami Beach. When I ran on a rent control platform, he stopped supporting me and broke off our friendship. I tried to explain to him that it was never going to pass, but he didn't believe me. I regret losing that friendship but hope that he eventually realized I was telling him the truth. I did what I thought was best for the city.

My journey as commissioner was just beginning, and the challenges and opportunities continued to shape my path forward. The memories of those early days in office would stay with me, serving as valuable lessons as I navigated the twists and turns of public service.

JUDGE

---

*I*N 1971, THE GOVERNOR OF FLORIDA WAS RUNNING FOR reelection. As a Republican in a Democratic state, he was predicted to lose the election in what most people were assuming would be a spectacular defeat. But he was still campaigning and he called the mayor of Miami Beach, asking the mayor to introduce him to six or seven Democratic groups when he was in the area. The mayor, understandably, refused. However, even though he would not do it himself, he did instruct his secretary to ask all the other commissioners to take the governor around town.

Not surprisingly, no one accepted the job.

No one but me.

At the time, I was the youngest commissioner and maybe it was my naiveté or my inexperience, but regardless of my colleagues calling me an idiot – after all, you don't want to campaign with the losing candidate – I volunteered.

I spent the day with the governor, showing him around Miami Beach and introducing him to various Democratic clubs. When the day was over, we went back to City Hall where he thanked me.

"You have some pretty big *cojones* for taking me around today," he said as he shook my hand.

I laughed but reassured him. "You're my governor," I said. "Glad to do it."

It was no shock that he lost the election. But with six weeks left to his term's official end, he used his last opportunity to fill empty positions for judges all around the state. The wife of the city doctor was a judge in the Industrial Claims court, and the governor was promoting her to a different court. That would leave her previous seat vacant, and I was a lawyer who practiced the same type of law. As it turns out, her husband, the city doctor, had also been my children's pediatrician. I went to visit him and told him that I would like to take his wife's position.

I also told him to remind the governor that I was the one who showed him around Miami Beach when no one else would.

He made the call to the governor and I was appointed as a judge.

This small story is remarkable to me for multiple reasons.

The chain of events that had to be in place in order for me to become a judge is seemingly random. However, each event relied on the previous event to get me to that appointment.

I chose to introduce a Republican governor to Democratic clubs – a job no one wanted or was foolhardy enough to take.

The doctor's wife practiced the same type of law that I was practicing at the time: workers' comp law.

She was promoted and there was a vacancy, right when I was

looking to become a judge. It was fortuitous timing, as I was not interested in running for reelection and wasn't even thinking of becoming mayor.

And finally, she was married to the city doctor and my children's pediatrician.

At the time, I attributed everything to just coincidence.

But in looking at the chain of events, I feel that there was a higher power involved that put me in the right place at the right time, making decisions that were simply unbelievable in allowing me to move up the ladder of success.

MEDICAL MYSTERIES

---

*W*HEN I WAS YOUNGER, I SPENT MANY DAYS BEING SICK.
As a result, I was pretty familiar with doctors and specialists. I was
also familiar with the arrogance that doctors have, particularly
when they couldn't find a cause or a cure for what ailed me.

When I was 17, I was home for close to a week with a high fever.
The fever hovered between 101 and 102, and so I was taking
whatever medicine they were giving me. But my throat stayed sore,
my glands swollen. After a week my temperature spiked to 104. By
the time I arrived at the hospital, it was over 105. My grandfather,
my uncles, and my parents were all there. The doctors packed me in
ice to try and break the fever and called in specialists. I remember
my mother crying and everyone around me praying. But something
else happened that day as well.

As I was shivering and burning up from the fever, I experienced
something that I could not fully explain. Even now, as I tell this
story, it seems so illogical, yet at the time it was clear. It made
perfect sense. I told my mother, who was standing next to me in
tears, that she needed to call her father and ask him to pray for me.

Somehow, I had received a "message" – a strong sign, clear as a bell amid all the chaos at the hospital – that my grandfather needed to pray for me.

My grandfather was a deeply spiritual man who woke up every day at 3:00 a.m. to study the Torah. He was poor and worked cleaning and running the *mikvah*, the ritual bath, in Williamsburg. I wasn't even sure if he even ever answered the phone.

But something told me that he needed to pray for me. My mother was panicked and when I told her what I felt needed to be done; she became more frazzled. But she did what I said.

My grandfather answered the phone and told my mother that he was going to synagogue and was going to pray for me that second. He told her to tell me not to worry. Regardless of his words, I went to sleep that night certain that I was not going to survive.

The next morning, I woke up and my fever had broken. My glands were completely normal, and my throat was fine. It was as if I had not even been sick. The doctors at the hospital had no explanation for what had happened. It seemed like a miracle.

I don't know why I had that idea of calling my grandfather that day in the hospital, I don't know how it came into my head that that was what I needed to do, but I also know unequivocally that his prayers helped to save me that day. It wasn't the first time something like that had happened, where I was gripped by an inexplicable message to do something that seemed almost nonsensical, and it certainly was not the last.

I remember one time when I went to the dentist for a toothache. After taking some X-rays and assessing the angry tooth, the dentist told me I needed a root canal. But days after that procedure, I was still in agony. The tooth throbbed. I couldn't do anything to stop the pain.

The dentist tried to investigate. He removed the root and tried to do the procedure another time. I sat in the chair as he dug into that tooth and left hoping the pain would subside.

It didn't.

I was in agony. Clearly, there was a problem that was not being addressed. I returned to the dentist and told him that the pain had not subsided. This time, the dentist was angry and frustrated. He had performed a root canal, he had revisited it, and still found nothing wrong. In frustration, he told me I should see an endodontist. From where he was sitting, there was nothing left to do.

The endodontist did the same thing the dentist had tried.

He removed the root, attempted to remove the nerve again, and then sealed the tooth. The pain did not go away. "The only thing we can do is pull the tooth," he said. This was horrifying to me and not something that I wanted to consider without looking at every possible option. That tooth was an anchor for the surrounding teeth. I wouldn't just lose a tooth. Pulling it would send me into a long process of implants and bridgework which I wanted to avoid. Additionally, I felt that the dentist was responsible! He had been digging around in that sensitive tooth. Maybe he just didn't want to deal with my pain and was looking for the easiest way out.

However, I was not a dentist. Or an endodontist. I agreed to the extraction.

He prepared me for the extraction, draping my body and opening the instruments he would need to pull my tooth. Something came over me though, and at the last minute, I asked him to stop.

"If the root has been removed, why do I still feel pain?" I asked him. "There has to be something else to try," I said. "Pulling the tooth can't be the only answer."

We argued and he agreed to try something a little out of the box.

He sent his nurse to a pharmacy to pick up a new medication. When she returned, he opened the tooth and put two drops into the cavity where the root had been. He instructed me to go home, take some codeine, and if it still hurt in the morning, it would be pulled.

Incredibly, by morning, I was no longer in pain.

As it turned out, all of that prodding and digging into my tooth traumatized my jawbone. It was never the tooth that was causing the pain, it was referred pain from the bone. Putting those steroid drops into the tooth calmed the nerves in my jaw, and the pain never returned.

It seems like a simple story, but it was important for me not to give in so quickly and take the easy way out. After all, it was my tooth! All the doctor needed was someone to give him a new way to look at things, and I was that person.

I wasn't a specialist in teeth, but at that time, I felt like I knew more than the specialist. That happened again, 20 years later with a medical situation that no doctor could explain.

For two years I had been suffering what looked like heart attacks. It first started when I was in a restaurant and suddenly started having severe chest pain. I went to the hospital and was admitted. Despite multiple tests, the doctors could not find anything wrong with me.

While most people would be happy with that news – and initially I was – these attacks continued every two to three months. Each time, I arrived at the hospital, they would examine me, find nothing conclusive, and release me. My doctor prescribed some medication, but it did not stop the attacks.

Thus began a long journey of trying multiple treatments to stop these frightening and painful attacks. My doctor was stumped. I went to an orthopedic surgeon: nothing. I saw chiropractors, specialists: nothing. I took different medications: still nothing. My doctor finally suggested I meet with a psychiatrist, but I knew that this pain was not in my head. It was a real thing, and it was debilitating. At one point, I flew to Johns Hopkins for a special scan called a myelogram in which a dye is injected into the spinal cord to see if any nerves are compressed. Unfortunately, they injected me with too much dye and I had to stay bedridden for 10 days until it worked out of my system. Still, when the results came back, they found nothing that could be causing these symptoms.

It is difficult to articulate the magnitude of my frustration and also my fear. I knew what I was feeling, I knew the pain that continued to plague me, and yet I was constantly dismissed. Doctors threw their hands up, or worse, they patronized me and then gently suggested it was all in my head. I started to think that maybe I was losing my mind.

At this point, I was a workers' compensation judge. While my courtroom was usually filled with doctors testifying about injured employees, in one case the doctor who was on the stand was the head of a Children's Hospital in Miami. The attorney on the case questioned the doctor to prove that his client could have a disability even though nothing showed on X-rays and scans. According to the doctor, it is possible for someone to be in pain, to have severe limitations, and not have those symptoms appear on any scans or tests.

I listened to his testimony and realized that he was describing exactly what I was going through.

The next day, I made an appointment to see the doctor who testified. He was surprised to see me, but I explained my situation and commented on his testimony from my courtroom.

"Doc," I explained, "I have been to many specialists, and no one has been able to help me. When I heard how you described a man who can have a disability without any concrete proof, I felt that maybe you could help me."

He agreed to try. He asked me questions about my childhood and about my mother's experience in childbirth. He asked me questions that had nothing to do with the pain or the heart attack feelings I was constantly getting. I started to think I had wasted my time and that maybe the doctor was just crazy. Finally, though, he asked me about any previous injuries I may have sustained as a child. I mentioned that when I was 16 I was injured in a basketball game and tore ligaments which put me in a sling for six weeks. I told him about the medications, injections, and scans that I had and how nothing had helped.

When I finished, he looked at me with a smile and said, "Judge? I will cure you for around $8."

I was stunned. I also thought that maybe he was crazy. After all, I had been to top doctors and consulted with specialists, and now, after all that, I had a doctor who claimed he could cure me for $8. But I went along, promising to pay much more if he could cure me.

"No, you don't understand," he explained. "Go to a Sears Roebuck and buy a pull-up bar. Hang it in a doorway of your home and four times a day, hang from it for 30 seconds."

"That's it?" I asked.

"That's it."

He explained that the torn ligaments I suffered as a teen had developed scar tissue over the years. And since I wasn't playing basketball or getting much exercise as I aged, the skeletal structure of my body was pressing upon the scar tissue, causing me pain that mimicked a heart attack.

The chances of this doctor, Dr. Pedro Arroyo, walking into my courtroom to testify about a situation that paralleled my own is nothing short of a miracle.

Seven other judges could have heard that case, and he was a doctor who never had testified in court before! In that one encounter, a problem that no specialist, no hospital, and no world-renowned clinic could solve, was solved. Even I wasn't initially so sure that he could help me. But for some reason, I went for the appointment. I followed up. I sat in that office and answered ridiculous questions. And in the end, he gave me an answer and a solution that no one else thought of in all my consultations and appointments. Was it fate? Luck? Or something else?

I bought the bar at Sears Roebuck and never had another attack.

DESTINY AND DIAMONDS

*T*HE YEAR WAS 1979 WHEN OUR LIVES TOOK AN INCREDIBLE turn that would forever shape the course of our jewelry business. My wife, Joan, and her sister, Marcia, had taken a bold step into the world of jewelry sales. With the support of my uncle, who was involved in manufacturing exclusive pieces for Tiffany, they embarked on selling jewelry in the lobbies of kosher hotels. Their venture proved successful, and they soon expanded to a store on the second floor of one of the hotels, joining forces with a friend who sold women's clothing.

As the business thrived, I decided to travel with Joan to attend the largest jewelry show in the world, held in Milan, Italy. Following the show, we visited various wholesale showrooms until we came across a company named SIROM. Unfortunately, they refused to provide Joan with wholesale prices, citing her gender as the reason. Frustrated, Joan asked me to intervene and speak to a bookkeeper who wore a skull cap and only understood Yiddish. Though he couldn't assist us directly, he directed me to the company's boss, instructing me to locate the office marked "executivo."

I was walking down the hallway, looking for the office when I overheard a heated argument in Hungarian, the language my parents would use when they wanted to keep something private. I knocked on the door and walked in, handing the man behind the desk my business card identifying me as an attorney. I introduced Joan as a jeweler.

The man looked at my card and said, "You're an attorney, not a jeweler." I explained again that Joan was the jeweler.

"I'm Norman Ciment," I said.

Everything stopped. The other man looked at me and then slowly inquired about my lineage.

"Are you Leo, Louis, Morris, or Jack's son?" he asked. I revealed my identity as Jack's son, and to my astonishment, he introduced himself as David Lowy, my cousin. His mother was a Ciment.

David explained that though he had never been to Florida, he was familiar with my family's background and had been following their endeavors. He generously offered to assist Joan in her jewelry purchases, providing her with access to his wholesale prices and all his factories. David's support and guidance transformed Joan's business overnight, guaranteeing her purchases of up to $1 million. We couldn't believe the remarkable coincidence that brought us to this distant relative who turned out to be the catalyst for her success.

Over the next two decades, we shared countless wonderful experiences with David and his wife, Roz, as we traveled to Italy, Hong Kong, Bangkok, and Israel, exploring the jewelry markets and forging strong bonds with one another. Even more heartwarming are the *chagim*, Sabbaths, and *simchas* we shared with each other's families and which still continue to this day.

It was indeed a "DP" moment – a Destiny and Providence moment

– that brought us together and one I will cherish forever. Joan's company just celebrated its 47th anniversary.

Another serendipitous incident occurred during our time in Hong Kong that same year.

We stumbled upon a small factory with 11 workers, where the conditions were harsh, with no air-conditioning and temperatures reaching 105 degrees Fahrenheit. Despite the discomfort, Joan's keen eye for design led her to make suggestions to improve their jewelry pieces. The owner was receptive and brought in an artist to sketch her ideas, resulting in the transformation of four jewelry pieces within minutes. They were so impressed with Joan's creativity that they invited us to dinner.

At dinner, Joan continued to share her design ideas. They asked her to return the next day, leading to the creation of 34 unique pieces. The connection with the factory owner proved invaluable as he treated Joan as his best customer over the years. She continued to utilize the designs she had contributed to their collection, and their trust in her allowed her to pay for the jewelry after selling it. This partnership elevated Joan's jewelry line to new heights, making it one of the most sought-after designer collections in the New York market.

The fusion of David Lowy's connections and the fortuitous alliance with the Hong Kong factory elevated her jewelry store, Jewelers Choice, to unparalleled success. It was a testament to the incredible power of destiny and the profound impact that a single encounter can have on one's life and career.

The journey from that chance meeting in Milan to the company's continued prosperity was nothing short of extraordinary.

RABBI GROSS AND THE HEBREW ACADEMY

$\mathcal{R}$ABBI ALEXANDER GROSS, OF BLESSED MEMORY, WAS A great friend and a giant in the field of Jewish education. He founded the Hebrew Academy of Miami Beach, Florida, and initially nominated me to serve as president for one year only. However, he would not let me leave the position for another three years. In fact, I had to draft someone else to eventually take over my presidency.

It wasn't difficult for him to convince me to stay.

Our three sons were students in the school, and so I had a vested interest in the school's success. At the time, there were non-observant Jews who wanted to take over the administration of the school and change its philosophy. There were teachers who had been there for a long period of time who were not maintaining their professional development. Their teaching methods were outdated, and they refused to take classes for new certification. It was a difficult decision, but in order to deal with this awkward situation he asked me to let them go.

I understood the predicament he was in and sympathized. It is never easy to have to fire a friend.

I looked at my job as a privilege. It was necessary to keep the school on par with the public schools and to ensure that the education followed the high standards necessary for a competitive school. In the four years that I served as president, the Hebrew Academy produced some of the finest students. The school continued to grow over the years and many graduates continued to serve the Jewish community at the highest levels.

My cousin Larry was one such graduate who became a leading pulmonary doctor and a talented diagnostician who has kept me in good shape and solved all my health problems for the past 25 years. His son Ari followed in his footsteps and is currently the chief of the ICU unit at Mount Sinai Medical Center. Other distinguished graduates include the Galbut family, a pillar in the Miami Beach community. The school produced heart surgeons, medical doctors, attorneys, and dozens of other professionals in many business, medical, and educational fields.

Even though I was only president for four years, I remained involved with the school for years after. In fact, Joan and I, through our charitable foundation, recently donated a robotic tech center to the new high school building, bringing the world of innovation and technology to another generation of students.

Leading the school for those years was one of my proudest moments, and I feel those days of collaborating with Rabbi Gross for the future of Jewish education still resonate today in the halls of the Hebrew Academy.

MAYOR AND *ERUV*

I DIDN'T EXPECT TO BECOME THE FIRST ORTHODOX JEWISH mayor in the United States. My religiousness and my commitment to the Torah and the commandments were always what guided my life. Becoming mayor was the culmination of a series of events that pushed me into that position.

In 1974, the city of Miami Beach was trapped by a moratorium on building and renovations on properties in South Beach. The entire South Beach area was in a state of disrepair and degradation. To add to that, Fidel Castro, through a deal with President Jimmy Carter, sent 100,000 Cuban refugees, many of whom were criminals from Cuban prisons, to settle in Miami. Miami Beach became known as the murder capital of the United States, and everyone wanted to see changes.

As a citizen, I was watching the destruction of my city and wanted changes. Property owners were trapped as they could not fix their properties. I tried to have the commission lift the moratorium, but they would not. Most of the men involved in that decision had a vested interest in keeping a ban on new construction. Five years had passed. It was 1979 and people were going bankrupt and losing their properties.

However, a good friend of mine and fellow attorney, Murray Meyerson, wanted to run for mayor. I told him I would back him and help him raise money if he agreed to lift the moratorium as soon as he was sworn in. Meyerson agreed and I got to work.

I wanted that moratorium lifted as much as the constituents, and so I put my name out there when I was raising money for Meyerson, promising that when he wins, he would lift the moratorium and allow the owners to repair and construct new buildings. Property owners trusted me and supported Meyerson, the candidate they believed would save the city.

And Meyerson won!

The victory was short-lived for me though. Even though he had campaigned on the solid ticket of lifting the moratorium, once he was in office, he was pressured by Steve Muss of the Fontainebleau who still believed that the big insurance companies would give him the financing. Muss wanted the project to remain because it involved 240 acres of land and would allow him to build a whole new city in South Beach.

Politics is a dirty game. I know that.

I had put my name on the line and even though I spoke on Meyerson's behalf, the voters who donated came to me. They were hurting financially and demanded what I had promised. I was in a very bad position. They blamed me.

I met with Meyerson and told him he must vote to lift the moratorium at the next meeting. If not, I was going to run against him in the next mayoral race to prove to the people I had solicited that I was a man of my word. At the next meeting, he did not even show up. He was in the hospital with "pain" which I knew was fake. My decision to run for this nonpartisan position was easy.

I launched my campaign and based it on lifting the crippling moratorium that was preventing the city from becoming a tourist destination and a profitable environment for investors.

It was not an easy race. Meyerson was backed by some of the wealthiest companies as well as every hotel association and the Miami Herald. The contest was going to be bitter. I hired Pat Caddell, the former publicist for Jimmy Carter, and after analyzing the race, he came back with a new campaign strategy.

His advice was to not insult Meyerson. He told me, "Don't attack him. Don't even say his name. Run on statistics and facts instead." This went against everything I believed about winning a race, but I trusted him. We shifted our strategy.

We advertised the growing rates of robberies, rapes, and murder. We painted a picture of how far the city had sunk with Meyerson in office without ever mentioning his name. I didn't fully agree but in the end, Caddell was right and I was wrong.

I followed his advice and won the election.

One of the reasons the crime rate was so high was due to the influx of Cuban refugees – many of whom were criminals. I was adamant that the city should not accept any more refugees without full prior knowledge of their backgrounds and history. It was obvious to me that we could not let criminals walk around on our streets indiscriminately.

In the end, I was correct. I was protecting the city and digging out from the terrible reputation it had received over the years. I was cleaning up the mess, and I was doing it successfully.

I immediately opened a jail that had been closed for 25 years. I hired 55 police officers and instructed them to arrest anyone who violated the law. The city began to turn around, and soon I created the second largest Art Deco District in the United States.

While I ran on a platform to help the city, there were still some people who were not pleased with my victory. One of those people was Steven Muss, the owner of the Fontainebleau Hotel. At an Independence Day party after the election, I stood next to him on a balcony of his penthouse apartment, looking down on the city.

"Ciment," he said, "you and your yarmulkas will ruin this city."

Without missing a beat, I replied, "Steve, I and the yarmulkas will save this city."

I ran on the platform of lifting the moratorium, but it wasn't so simple. At my first meeting, I was voted down 6 to 1. But I did not relent and continued to fight for what I felt was right. For the next nine months, I made the same motion, putting pressure on all my commissioners, telling them that I would campaign to defeat them if they did not change their vote. Finally, nine months later, at a commissioners' meeting, the vote to lift the moratorium passed 7 to 0. Immediately, work began to improve the city. The Art Deco District was created as well as a beautiful boardwalk.

I started this chapter by explaining that I didn't set out to be the first Orthodox Jewish mayor in America. But when I won the election, that role fell on my shoulders almost immediately.

A prominent rabbi, Rabbi Tibor Stern, came to meet me in my

office soon after the election. He didn't have an appointment. He came in, sat down, and said, "You weren't elected because you are good-looking or because you are a smart lawyer. You were elected so that you could build an *eruv* in Miami Beach for the Jewish community."

An *eruv* is a string that encircles a city or a particular area which allows Orthodox Jews to carry items outside their homes.

It was a nice thought, but I explained to Rabbi Stern that building an *eruv* around the city would cost at least $500,000. There was no way I was going to put this on my agenda.

The rabbi didn't flinch. "You'll figure it out," he said. "It is why you were elected." He then left my office.

His words stayed with me.

Three months later I was reading Time Magazine when I saw an article that proved to be prescient, even though I was not aware of it at the time. The article was about the Reichmann brothers, a religious Jewish family who owned multiple real estate developments. They ran into a problem with their workers.

The Reichmanns would not work on holidays and so the workers would also miss those days. But the workers felt it was unfair. After all, they were willing to work, they didn't keep the holidays, so why should they lose out on pay? They went so far as to put a sign on one of the unfinished buildings that read "The Jews are sucking our blood!" Reichmann needed to create a solution that was amenable to both sides. He met with union leaders and the general contractor and while they all agreed that Reichmann was correct, they needed to appease the angry workers. Reichmann knew the workers would listen to the archdiocese as they were religious church members. The church came up with a solution: they would extend the workers' hours during the week, pay them time and a half for those extra hours, and then when they were not paid for the holidays, the extra hours would balance out that loss. It was a perfect solution where both sides achieved their purposes. The workers agreed and they even put a new sign on the building, apologizing for what they had previously written.

When I read the article, I didn't think about it. But later that same week, I had a situation that was similar. The city workers' union wanted more money and more benefits. The Reichmann article and the words of Rabbi Stern suddenly crystallized and provided me with a solution.

I spoke to the union representatives and really yelled at them. I asked, "Why do you always ask for more and more? What is it that you have done for the city that entitles you to ask for more all the time?" They were shocked that the mayor was yelling at them. I wanted to drive home the idea that they should go above and beyond in order to get more from the city.

"What do you want us to do?" they asked.

This was where Reichmann's idea played out.

"I want the city to donate the use of six cherry picker trucks. I want you to drive them and let the Jews string up the *eruv* around the city. In exchange, I'll let those drivers work at the convention center and will pay them overtime for their work."

Building the *eruv* was an extraordinary accomplishment and changed the face of Miami Beach forever. Suddenly, it was a viable vacation spot for many Jewish people. It also became a place where Jews could see themselves living. As the *eruv* went up, the Jewish community began to grow, bringing new businesses and restaurants to cater to this new demographic.

Becoming the mayor started out as a way to retain my good name and lift the moratorium. I didn't realize at the time that stepping into that place in city hall was also putting me in a place of history, creating one of the most important first steps in triggering the growth of the Jewish community in South Florida.

Even more extraordinary is the series of events that led up to it.

When Rabbi Stern walked into my office and said, "This is why you became the mayor," I didn't fully understand the importance of my role. Regardless, I learned that I was just the conduit for this to take place. Someone else was pulling the strings, putting me into the position to run for mayor, handing me an article that would give me a solution to a local problem which in turn would allow me to build the *eruv*.

That entire series of events is nothing short of remarkable. It was the hand of a higher power, making it possible to solve a situation I never thought could be solved without spending a large amount of money.

Years later, the city was booming and Steven Muss's only granddaughter became engaged to an Orthodox Jewish man who happened to be my cousin. At the wedding, I saw Steven Muss and recalled our conversation on the roof of his building the summer after I became mayor.

"Steve," I said, "I'm so happy to see you and witness you joining the family of yarmulkes." It took him a few moments until he remembered our conversation. Shaking my hand, he looked at me and smiled. At that moment, I was sure I felt God winking at me.

BRICKMAN AND THE *KASHRUT* INDUSTRY

*I*N THE EARLY 1960S, MY FATHER SERVED AS PRESIDENT OF the local synagogue, where Rabbi Rackovsky was responsible for overseeing *kashrut* throughout the community. However, there was an unsettling collaboration between the rabbi and the city inspector, Frank Brickman, who held the role of chief inspector for *kashrut* in the city. Their involvement in various situations raised eyebrows and sparked curiosity.

Among those affected by this questionable alliance was Phil Weiss, a close friend of my father and the owner of the renowned Royal Hungarian restaurant. The city inspector seemed to have a knack for causing Phil trouble with constant inspections and nitpicking. Frustrated by this apparent abuse of power, my father and Phil hatched a plan to establish a *vaad*, a council that would replace the Rabbi in ruling on all *kashrut* matters presented by the inspector.

However, this move didn't sit well with the inspector, and he did not hesitate to make his displeasure known. He called my father, issuing a veiled threat, warning him to stop meddling in *kashrut* affairs and prioritize the well-being of his family and business. Undeterred, my father and Phil Weiss stood their ground and proceeded with the formation of the *vaad*.

The tension between my father's *vaad* and the inspector escalated when, in the early 80s, I represented the largest kosher caterer in Miami Beach. I advised them to refrain from offering any free meals or money to the inspector, urging caution in their dealings with him. Unfortunately, their caution couldn't protect them from a peculiar incident that would make headlines.

One day, they were arrested and taken to jail in handcuffs after the inspector found a case of non-kosher soup base in their pantry. The case had not been opened, and it turned out that a food broker had mistakenly delivered the non-kosher soup base instead of the kosher one that was ordered.

Victor's Soup Company had two sources coming from two different cities, one of which was kosher and the other which was not. It was a simple unintentional mix-up from the company.

I tried to explain the situation to Mr. Brickman, but he was unwavering in his pursuit of prosecution. He went to the state attorney's office to try and convict my clients and make sure they lost their catering contracts.

The case went to trial, and it made headlines in the Miami Herald. Their key witness was a rabbi in Miami Beach whose son had ambitions of taking over the catering business from the two partners. My key witness was Rabbi Stern, the one who told me I would build the *eruv*. The trial involved intricate Jewish laws that needed explanation to the gentile judge presiding over the case.

Ultimately, the judge ruled in favor of the caterers, stating that the mistake was not intentional and that the caterer did not violate the kosher laws, especially since he never used the soup base. Additionally, even if the soup had been used, there is a *kashrut* law that says if a non-kosher ingredient is less than 1/60th of a particular food, the food is still considered kosher, even if that small amount was mixed in with the food.

This loss was a significant blow to the inspector, who was livid. He attributed his defeat to the involvement of a politician, meaning me, as their attorney. It was the only case he ever lost in his 27-year tenure as the city inspector. A few years later, the city abolished the position entirely and the *vaad* took over. I couldn't help but think that my father would have been delighted with the outcome.

In a twist of fate, before the inspector's position was abolished, I was invited by Brickman along with Rabbi Irving Lehrman, who presided over the magnificent Temple Emanu-El in Miami Beach, to a kosher dinner at the prestigious Fontainebleau Hotel. That memorable evening included an unforgettable performance by none other than the legendary Frank Sinatra, who sang "Happy Birthday" to me no less!

This highlighted a chapter of ups and downs in the *kashrut* industry, where Divine Providence seemed to guide the course of events, often in unexpected ways.

MIAMI HERALD

$\mathcal{T}$HE MIAMI HERALD WAS THE MOST WIDELY READ PAPER in South Florida and for some reason, they did not like me. I am not saying this facetiously or tongue-in-cheek. I was always at the center of any negative press they could find. It wasn't just that they didn't endorse me – that's the nature of politics – it was that they never even gave me the courtesy of an interview which they gave to every other candidate. Whenever they could twist a story to create bad press, they did. If there was a positive story, they ignored it and didn't report on it. It seemed as if they wanted to bury Miami Beach in a sea of misinformation and negativity.

In 1981, it was easy to do.

Thanks to Fidel Castro and President Carter, thousands of criminals poured into Miami Beach, filling the city with drug dealers, addicts, and former sanatorium residents. It was a city that was later memorialized in *Scarface*. This was the city I inherited when I became mayor.

Three weeks into my term, the editor of the Miami Herald came to my office. He didn't have an appointment. He informed my office staff that he was on his way and wanted a meeting with me.

If I had thought he was coming to congratulate me, I was quickly proven wrong. Instead of congratulating me on my recent win, he started berating me about the crime in Miami Beach. His concern was about the city of Miami proper. Rising crime rates in Miami Beach translated into lower tourism rates in Miami. According to him, I needed to do something about it in order to save the image of Miami.

I decided to turn the tables on him. After all, this was a man who never endorsed me, never said a positive word about me, and did not care about the city I represented.

"You tell me," I began. "What do you think I should do to clear up the crime?"

"You need to hire an additional six police officers and start cleaning up the city." He made that suggestion even though he knew full well that our budget was tight. Regardless, I knew what I was doing.

"Six police officers," I said. "Let's see what we can do about that." I picked up my phone and called my secretary.

"I need the chief of police immediately. Please call him and tell him to come to my office right away. He should make sure to use his lights and sirens to get here as quickly as possible."

The chief was only a few blocks away, so within a minute or so, the sirens could be heard blaring through the streets of Miami Beach. A few minutes later he was in my office, wondering what the problem was.

I looked at the police chief and repeated what the editor of the paper had told me. I told the chief about the concerns, about the rising crime rate, and I also told him what the editor had proposed.

"Please," I told him, "can you tell our editor what happened after I was installed as mayor of Miami Beach?"

The chief sat down in one of my chairs, looked squarely at the editor, and proceeded to detail what transpired after I became mayor.

"Mayor," he began, "you were installed at 10 a.m. That same afternoon, we met right in this office, and you instructed me to hire 55 new police officers. They were to be placed all over the city. You wanted a motorcycle squad to police the alleyways and policemen on horseback to patrol the avenues. You ordered 12 officers to be placed on every corner in South Beach with batons to keep the criminals and the vagrants at bay. Additionally, you opened the police station that had been closed for 23 years and put the word out that criminals will be prosecuted to the full extent of the law."

The editor was dumbstruck and didn't know what to say, but rather than thank me, he got up and said, "We will be watching you," before leaving the office.

One year later we had a convention of 500 travel agents coming to Miami Beach to promote the area and see our new $80-million beach and the new hotels. After I had lifted the seven-year moratorium and allowed all the owners to redo their buildings, I hoped we were going to sell them on our beautiful city and recharge the tourism industry in Miami Beach.

Our main meeting was scheduled for a Monday.

In Sunday's Miami Herald, in the Neighbors section, a weekly magazine section that highlights different neighborhoods, there was a front-page article listing the worst beaches in the U.S. The entire centerfold was about the disaster in Miami Beach. Instead of the upgraded beaches, they displayed gravel and pavement, rocks and dark sand. It was a disaster.

I was furious.

They did this on purpose because their goal was to make Miami Beach an old community and wanted Miami to be the top spot. The equation was simple: ruin Miami Beach to build up Miami.

In 24 hours, I had to greet the travel agents and convince them that the article was false. I ordered my staff to reprint the article in a small pamphlet. Then, I wrote a scathing letter and sent 40,000 copies to all registered voters and businesspeople in Miami Beach to let them know that the Miami Herald was destroying their businesses, hotels, and restaurants on the one week that 500 travel agents were coming to visit us. I encouraged them to cancel their ads and stop supporting the paper.

The civic league, the chamber of commerce, and all the businesspeople agreed with me. They canceled ads and subscriptions to the Miami Herald. The Herald asked the chamber of commerce to "Stop the crazy mayor!" They answered, "We can't do anything because everyone agrees with him."

The Herald hated me more than ever, but the people of Miami Beach and the people I represented loved me more than ever. The Herald requested a meeting where they apologized for printing the article when they did.

Lifting the moratorium, creating the Art Deco District, building a new city hall, a new marina, and new boardwalk, and building the *eruv* – all of these set the city on a roll. I saw a problem and went to attack it. My priority was always my city and my citizens, and in this case – even with them trying to tear everything down – I beat them.

That's what makes a good politician. That's what makes a solid leader.

BEN GRENALD

*I*N 1982, MY FRIEND BEN GRENALD, A FORMER CITY commissioner, wanted to serve on a city board. He told me he had three solid votes for the position and asked me if I would be his fourth vote. He was a good friend and highly qualified. I had no problem supporting him, but something about his surety in the other three votes did not sit right with me. I told him that if he had three votes, I would definitely be the fourth one, but I also listened to that nagging suspicion about the other votes. I decided to investigate.

Sure enough, I discovered that the commissioners who had guaranteed Ben their votes had lied. They knew that I was going to vote for him, and so they wanted to ensure he would not get the position. I knew I needed to tell Ben what was happening behind the scenes, but I also knew that he probably would not believe me. At worst, maybe he would think I was telling him these things in order to back out of the commitment I gave to vote for him.

I was right. When I told Ben about what was going to happen, he didn't believe me. He accused me of lying. It put me in a difficult decision. I knew that I was going to be the only person voting for him at the end, and a part of me thought that I should just not vote. After all, he was going to lose. Plus, he accused me of lying to him.

In the end, I decided my friendship with him was more important than looking like a fool. I told Ben I would vote for him to prove to him that I never lie, even though he would only have one vote – my vote. I wanted to show him that my word was truly my bond.

He still could not believe that the other commissioners would not keep their promises and was sure he would be appointed. In fact, he decided to sit in the front row during the vote.

As I predicted, they did not vote his way. The vote was presented five times. The three other commissioners staggered their votes so that all three never voted at the same time. At the final vote, I was the only one voting for Ben. I was the lone voter, but I wouldn't break my word to my friend.

Ben Grenald became my business partner and never doubted my word again. We had been friends prior, but at that moment, we were bonded by faith and honesty. We continued to work together and created numerous business deals which turned into lucrative opportunities,

Even though it was embarrassing that the mayor backed a losing candidate, I proved to everyone watching that day that I was a man of integrity and honor.

My partnership with Ben Grenald continued for many years. I like to think that the secret to our success was simple: I kept my word.

SANTA MARTA, COLOMBIA

*I*N 1982, THE CITY OF SANTA MARTA, COLOMBIA, WAS THE
sister city of Miami Beach.

As mayor, I was invited to judge Santa Marta's beauty pageant.
It was like the Miss America pageant of Colombia. I knew it
was important as a dignitary to participate and so I accepted the
invitation. However, the event was scheduled to take place on
Saturday. I explained to the organizers that because of the Sabbath
I would be unable to drive to the event and asked if they could
house me at a hotel within walking distance of the hall.

There was definitely some confusion on their part, but the primary
goal of being closer to the event was achieved. However, instead
of being in a hotel nearby, they put me up in a private residence
owned by an important local businessman who was also a deacon
in one of the largest churches in the area.

His name was Abraham Infante, and even though we were from two
different worlds, we struck up a unique friendship that weekend.
He was a devout Christian – there were statues of Jesus above all
the beds in the home – but his ancestors, incredibly, were Jewish.
Through years of intermarriage, no one was Jewish anymore, but
his family had tremendous pride in their heritage. As such, most of

his extended family retained Hebraic names from the Torah. I met many of his family members who traced their roots back to Spanish Marranos, secret Jews who kept their Jewish identity during the Spanish Inquisition. Like my host, Abraham, though they were all Christian, they held their Jewish past in high esteem and were proud of their heritage.

The pageant I was judging was a major event in Santa Marta. Over 15,000 people were in the audience as well as thousands more outside the venue. The building I slept in was guarded by soldiers who stood in front and on neighboring rooftops. It was an enormous undertaking for the city and clearly an important event.

Even though I was staying close to where the pageant was happening, I was still a mile away. On Saturday morning, I reminded my hosts that I was going to walk to the event, despite the 95-degree heat. To my absolute shock, every member of the household had decided that they would walk with me. Even though they were able to avoid the oppressive heat and take their own cars, they wanted to walk together. I don't know if it was because of the connection they felt to their generations past or if they were just being respectful, but either way, we were a sight to behold. Two hundred soldiers accompanied us on that walk to the pageant and we were quite the entourage.

As far as the beauty pageant was concerned, I played it safe. Santa Marta was the capital city for marijuana, and the cartel controlled the army and the police. So I asked them who they wanted to win, and I voted for that contestant. Overall, I would say that everyone was thrilled with the way the weekend worked out, and when I returned home, I organized a shipment of several hundred thousand dollars' worth of old medical equipment for the local hospital.

Observing the Sabbath created a connection with my hosts in the least likely way. I connected to a family of Christians and a community of non-Jews through our shared pasts. It was a glorious experience.

CANNES FILM FESTIVAL

*T*HERE ARE TIMES WHEN I LOOK BACK AT OCCURRENCES in my life and marvel at how certain elements lined up at the right time to allow me to experience an astonishing moment of synchronicity. This story is one of those moments which may seem trivial and the result of uncanny coincidence, but one that I feel has greater power.

I was traveling with Joan in Milan, Italy, to assist her in buying jewelry for her store. As luck would have it, our plans for the weekend had fallen through, and so we were looking for a place to stay. Some jewelers suggested that we travel to Nice, which was only a few hours away. The Cannes film festival – the largest film festival in Europe – was taking place then. Our friends told us to find a hotel out of the city, as all hotels would be booked for the event, and then spend Saturday night and Sunday going to the festival. It seemed like a great idea and we started on our way.

About 30 miles out of the city, I started stopping at hotels to see if there was a vacancy. Every single hotel was booked. I drove everywhere. I took backroads and side streets. But no matter what place I found, there were no rooms available.

The hours were ticking away and the Sabbath was coming. I had driven into the city and made the decision that we would need to buy food and live in our car for the weekend. There was simply no availability.

However, something stopped me.

I can't explain why or what motivated me, but I told Joan that I was going to walk into the main hotel in Cannes and try and get a room. It was a crazy idea and there was no reason to think that I would be successful, especially with the previous few hours of trying every hotel in a 30-mile radius. I knew it was a futile effort, but I figured that at worse, we could sleep in the hotel lobby instead of our car. It was worth a shot.

The hotel was packed with people. There were celebrities from all over the world and paparazzi and fans everywhere I looked. I walked through the throngs to the front desk and without saying a word, I handed over my passport and said I was there to check in.

I braced myself for the rejection.

It never came.

Instead, the woman at the desk handed me papers to sign and a key to a room. In a performance worthy of one of the films at the festival, I hid my shock and merely said thank you.

I went to the room with Joan and once we were in our room instructed her not to open the door if anyone knocks. I assumed the hotel would realize their mistake and try and have us leave.

That knock never came and we were able to spend our Sabbath there.

I found out later that there was a major movie producer from Paris named Marcel Ciment who had reserved a block of rooms for all of his people who traveled to Cannes to see his film. I left a note for him and asked to meet, but he never reached out. Interestingly, I met his aunt and cousins in Paris the following year. They were distant cousins of ours who survived the war by moving to Paris and never changed their name.

That weekend at Cannes was incredible. We were able to attend many foreign film premieres as well as a screening of *Chariots of Fire*, which went on to win an Oscar for Best Picture later that year.

I can't explain why I walked into the busiest, most exclusive hotel in Cannes and attempted to get a room. I also can't explain how the one hotel that I chose happened to have had a producer with my same last name on a block of reservations. Everything had been set up for Joan and me to observe the Sabbath in a hotel during one of the most prestigious film events in the world.

It may sound simple, but to me, this was a moment that I can only describe in one word: *divine.*

DOLPHINS IN NEW YORK

*I*T WAS THE EARLY 1980S AND THE MIAMI DOLPHINS were playing the New York Jets in a major game.

This wasn't a small moment; it was monumental. Football fans tend to be rabid and the amount of local pride among fans and those who don't even follow football was at an all-time high.

I wanted to embrace this moment and solidify Miami's place on the national stage. However, instead of supporting our team from Miami, I decided to do it from the lion's den. I flew to New York City where the game was going to be played.

Prior to my visit, I contacted the mayor of New York and told him my plan. He helped spread the word and had articles written about my visit in most of the newspapers in the city. I also wanted to make my presence known personally.

The weather in New York was hovering somewhere around 20 degrees and there was snow on the ground, but that didn't stop me. I zipped up the coat I had borrowed from my cousin, put on some warm gloves, and walked down Orchard Street holding a sign inviting all New Yorkers to come to visit sunny Miami Beach! It was an opportune time to carry that sign and walk around as I am sure most people were wishing they were out of the cold!

Everything was in place to celebrate the Miami Dolphins' win in New York City. I was staying in a suite in the Waldorf Astoria which was going to be the main site of the victory party.

I had sent 5,000 balloons to be released above Central Park with prizes attached to 1,000 of them for free hotel rooms in Miami. When the Dolphins won, we planned a parade down the East Side complete with swimsuit models in fur coats, handing orange juice out to the spectators.

It was going to be a colossal event and a major PR moment for Miami.

At the half-time mark, Miami was leading 7 to 0. My suite was packed with reporters from all over the world who were eating and drinking, ready for the celebration to really explode at the end of the game.

But unfortunately, our luck ran out. By the end of the third quarter, Miami was trailing. By the end of the game, Miami had lost. My celebratory suite had emptied out towards the end of the game with reporters itching to get a story from the winning team instead of staying with the loser.

It would have been incredible to have won that year, but I still didn't regret the hype and excitement that led up to the loss. It was a fine moment for Miami, and even with the loss, we still were making noise and promoting tourism to the South.

However, I admit I made a mistake. I should have still had the parade and released the 5,000 balloons.

I regret it to this day!

SIMON WIESENTHAL

*T*HERE ARE MANY STORIES ABOUT MY TIME AS MAYOR. One of the stories that I am particularly proud of was when my city hosted a world premiere of Simon Wiesenthal's award-winning documentary, *Genocide*, produced by RabbMarvin Hier of the Simon Wiesenthal Foundation and narrated by Elizabeth Taylor and Orson Welles.

I'm not sure how the idea originated, but I know it began to take shape when the mayor of Vienna came to visit Miami Beach. She was touring the United States and her arrival in Miami Beach was a great public relations moment for the city. I made sure to wine and dine her, showing her around the city on a private tour, and providing her with tickets for shows and reservations at our best restaurants. When it was time for her to leave, she invited me to visit her in Vienna. I took her up on the offer.

I went to Vienna with some friends and remembered that Simon Wiesenthal, the famous Nazi hunter, lived in Vienna. At the time, he had just finished production on his new documentary, *Genocide*. It was a controversial film, primarily because it took a critical stance against the Pope in 1942 and his failure to assist the Jews in Europe. I wanted to bring Wiesenthal to Miami Beach for the premiere of that film. And since I was in Vienna, it was a perfect opportunity to make the overture and extend the invite.

We met at my hotel in Vienna and spoke for over two hours. It was a fascinating conversation and it was exciting to meet him in person. More importantly, he agreed to show his film in Miami Beach.

I wanted this event to be huge – a moment when Miami Beach would be in the national spotlight. My friend Ron Molko helped me coordinate the visit, opening his home in Miami Beach where we held a welcome party for Simon Wiesenthal. I rented the largest theater on Lincoln Road and created a Hollywood-type event. There were massive searchlights illuminating the sky, visible for miles from the premiere, and a lavish red carpet for the dignitaries and guests. Over 2,000 people showed up for the event with many left standing outside just trying to get a glimpse of Wiesenthal. I had hoped for an event that would create good publicity for Miami Beach and I got more than that. The night was covered internationally, with countries across the globe commenting on the fanfare and beauty surrounding the premiere.

Wiesenthal never let any of that go to his head. He was a class act.

In fact, organizations and Jewish groups reached out to him when he was in Miami Beach in order to meet him and discuss other events. But his response that week, whenever he received a phone call or request, was always the same.

"Gentlemen," he said, "this man came to Vienna to personally invite me. I am his guest and will remain with him for the entirety of my visit."

And stay with me he did. It was a glorious week of parties and meetings. Having Simon Wiesenthal come to Miami Beach still remains one of the highlights of my career.

MAKING REAL ESTATE "REAL"

$\mathcal{R}$EAL ESTATE DEALS HAVE A UNIQUE WAY OF SHAPING destinies.

It isn't just the destiny of the buyer and seller. In my experience, the real estate I invested in transformed not only my own life but the face of entire communities.

One of the most valuable lessons I learned was from a Canadian man who came from the same town in Hungary as my father. He had a thick Hungarian accent and we instantly connected over our shared heritage. He was bidding on the same buildings as my firm but outbid us by a significant amount of money. We discussed the properties afterward and I told him what our bid was. He said, "You made a mistake. You didn't look at these properties the right way."

Naturally, I was taken aback. After all, I had been in the real estate industry for some time, and I liked to think I knew what I was doing.

"You bid correctly," he continued, "because you looked at the property through a microscope. Right now, your bid reflects the value of the property as it stands. But me, I always look through a telescope. I look at what the future of the property will be."

It was a powerful lesson that solidified through our partnership. He asked me to become his partner and buy into the buildings we had both bid on. I did some research and it turned out that he was one of the largest real estate owners in Toronto and clearly knew what he was doing. I convinced my partners and we put up the money to own a stake in the buildings.

Looking at real estate through a telescope rather than a microscope changed my life and transformed my investment strategies. It allowed me to be focused on the future instead of the "now" and envision growth where others could not see it.

I used that strategy from that day forward.

In the early 90s, two groups approached me with an ambitious plan to purchase three separate buildings in Miami Beach, totaling 850 units on Collins Avenue. These buildings were all rentals, but the groups had a vision to convert them into condominiums. What made this venture particularly fascinating was the fact that both groups were made up of Orthodox Jewish individuals. To secure the necessary secondary financing, they partnered with an older group of Orthodox Jewish investors who had deep connections with Orthodox families up North.

Their relationships proved fruitful when they managed to presell about 75 apartments to these families before even finalizing the purchase. As the conversion took place, it created a significant change in the entire area from 35th to 55th Street on Collins Avenue. Many other buildings followed suit, adding synagogues to cater to the growing Orthodox community.

I saw a golden opportunity in this transforming neighborhood – a need for a kosher restaurant to serve the residents of these new condominiums.

That's when I crossed paths with Bonnie Poon, chef at the Eden Roc Hotel.

I loaned him money to buy a condominium to be used as a kosher restaurant, and it became an overwhelming success. Over time, he expanded and opened another restaurant in upstate New York. The development of this area and the success of Bonnie's restaurant were remarkable outcomes of this real estate deal, showcasing the power of vision and strategic partnerships.

But not all of my real estate deals were as lucrative.

In fact, there is one deal that never came to fruition which I still think about.

For 35 years, every real estate deal brought to our firm had been a profitable investment, but as they say, there's an exception to every rule. In 1995, just after my retirement, I stumbled upon an extraordinary office building on 16th and Michigan Avenue. The bank had foreclosed on the property, and I secured a contract to purchase it for a mere $1.25 million. The building boasted four stories of parking and approximately 60,000 square feet of office space, with an additional empty lot at the corner.

Excitement was building as I envisioned the potential of this property, and my plan was to have my old firm move in as a tenant and help manage the building, which had about 40 percent vacancy. This strategic move could have been a game-changer, especially as Lincoln Road, just beginning to take off, would significantly boost the area's value.

However, the unfortunate twist came when my partner, Marvin Weinstein, who had always relied on our judgment in real estate matters, decided to say no.

Despite their lack of experience in real estate, the other partners agreed with Weinstein and made the one decision that would haunt us. We never purchased the building, and to my dismay, the parking lot that was part of the property turned into the most valuable piece in the area, consistently filled with tourists shopping on Lincoln Road.

Years later, the same building that I had the opportunity to buy for $1.25 million was sold for over $40 million. It was a heartbreaking reminder of the fickle nature of real estate deals and the one missed opportunity that I couldn't shake off. Despite our otherwise successful track record, this particular decision became the most significant regret in my real estate journey.

Real estate deals are an unpredictable blend of skill, timing, intuition, and *mazal* (luck).

While we celebrated the triumphs that transformed neighborhoods and enriched communities, we also learned the hard way about the cost of one wrong decision. Both experiences serve as valuable lessons and further reinforce the adage that every deal is a unique adventure with its own set of rewards and risks.

MEDIATION

$\mathcal{E}$very so often I find myself placed in a situation that I never planned and where I could never fathom the ultimate outcome. Becoming a mediator was one of those times.

I never believed in mediation and so I never wanted to pursue it. I thought it was a waste of time. Litigation and arbitration was the way to go. However, in 1985 I went to dinner with Judge Jason Berkman, who suggested that I register for a course to become a state mediator.

It really wasn't something I was interested in, so I thanked him for the suggestion and almost forgot about it. About two years later, though, it came up again. A fellow city commissioner, Mal Englander, mentioned to me in passing that he was going to West Palm Beach for four days to take a mediation course. The law was changing, and soon the requirements to become licensed were going to be more time-consuming and difficult. I decided to join him for the course.

It was almost like a small vacation. We took the classes and our wives spent the days shopping and enjoying West Palm. I finished the course and really didn't think that much of it. It was just another license to attach to my resume.

In 1995, I retired from my firm where I had practiced since 1963, and went into real estate with two friends. Out of the blue, I received a call from my tennis partner, Judge Alan Kuker, who was also the senior judge in the same court where I had served as a judge. He told me that the state was suddenly requiring all cases to go to mediation before trial. He was having a difficult time because the mediators were not proficient at their jobs. He wanted me to train them.

My mediation license was now something I was going to put to use. I had the time and the honor to be given that proposal.

I went back and worked for the state for almost a year and trained his people, working two days a week. In that time, I discovered that a good mediator could in fact make the parties settle without going to court. I was surprised by this because I had never really felt mediation was viable. Even though I eventually went back to real estate, I continued to work as a mediator three days a week over the next ten years. I conducted over 2,000 mediations and settled over 80 percent of those cases. I even conducted special request mediations on real estate and contested divorce cases.

It was one of the most gratifying and interesting times in my professional career. I was honored by an organization of attorneys practicing workers' compensation law at a wonderful dinner with over 400 people in attendance,

The most intriguing part of mediation was finding the elusive ingredient that makes it possible to get the parties to settle their differences. The difference between arbitration and mediation is an arbitrator renders a decision, but in mediation, you must get both parties to agree to settle, which is not an easy task. That challenge is what made the job exciting and interesting.

I never thought I would enjoy mediation and even scoffed a bit at the initial suggestion to take the course. But taking it and finding joy in the job was one of the high points of my career. I sincerely enjoyed it.

And all because of a random course that I never wanted to take!

This proves that you should sometimes take a second look at certain situations. I thank Judge Kuker for giving me that opportunity which resulted in one of the most gratifying periods of my life. We became very close friends and I convinced him to move to Miami Beach, where he and his family still reside.

ANSWERING TERROR

*I*N THE LATE 90S, ISRAEL FOUND ITSELF ENGULFED IN THE shadow of a second intifada, a relentless storm of attacks launched by Palestinian terrorists against civilians. Day after day, the citizens of Israel lived in fear as these civilian terrorists struck men, women, and children, targeting restaurants, public gatherings, weddings, school buses – any place where innocent civilians gathered. The havoc caused by these acts of terror rippled through the country, leaving death, injuries, and devastation in their wake. Tourists shied away from visiting Israel due to the prevailing insecurity, leading to soaring unemployment, plummeting businesses, and deserted shopping districts, where locals feared the prospect of being blown up by suicide bombers.

The crisis weighed heavily on my mind, and it reminded me of the tales my father shared about the Great Depression's impact on his thriving business in the United States back in 1930. My father wrote a letter to the newspaper with an idea about how to end the Depression. His idea was simple. He proposed a lottery every week where people could buy tickets for 10 cents. The prizes would be appliances and major items such as stoves, cars, and radios. This would allow the factories to start manufacturing the items for the prizes and in turn, the factories would need to hire workers.

I never forgot that letter.

Inspired by his resilience and determination, I pondered ways to make a difference in the face of this turmoil. And so, I set my sights on Israel.

I embarked on a journey to the heart of Israel, visiting its bustling cities and towns, and making it my mission to extend a helping hand.

My plan was to offer financial aid to various stores and businesses in the areas most affected by the senseless violence. I created coupons in $100 denominations that store owners signed for, and then took those coupons and gave them to people to shop at the different stores. It was like purchasing gift cards to each establishment. At first, the store owners were utterly bewildered by my proposal. They couldn't grasp the idea of this unusual project. But as I patiently explained, they began to warm up to it.

In each store, I offered to donate up to $500, requesting coupons of equal value in return. To my surprise, many storekeepers, touched by the cause, contributed even more, adding an extra 5 or 10 percent to their donations. With every step, the news of my mission spread like wildfire. People called the office of the local mayor, local news stations, and newspapers, all eager to know more about the family from Florida who had come to help.

For days, I walked through the bustling streets. I visited hospitals in Jerusalem where the victims were being treated. Meeting the injured and their families, I distributed the coupons, tailoring them to suit their needs based on family size and circumstances. They couldn't believe that this gesture was real. Through a Hebrew translator, I explained our intentions– simple Jewish people who felt the need to assist their fellow Jews.

Gratitude flowed like a river, tears of relief and joy mingling with blessings bestowed upon us.

Word of our endeavor reached the mayor's office, but even they struggled to fathom the scope of our compassion. Determined to make a difference, we requested a list of families impacted by the attacks, ensuring they would also receive the coupons we had to offer.

The media caught wind of our actions, and radio, television, and news outlets covered the story of the Florida family trying to make a difference in Israel. Our project brought a renewed sense of life to the areas that had fallen into desolation. The local families started patronizing the shops and businesses, restoring their vitality and bringing hope to the victims, their families, and the store owners.

It didn't stop there. Several years later, another project came about, one that would deeply impact thousands of struggling families in Israel. We discovered that numerous families were living in dire poverty, relying on welfare funds for food and subsidized rent. Many of these families were large, with five, six, or even seven children. The fathers worked menial jobs that barely sustained their day-to-day existence, while the mothers, after caring for their kids, would take up jobs as maids whenever possible. Their homes were equipped with outdated appliances – some using microwaves to heat food, others with 20-plus-year-old fridges and ovens with only one or two working burners. Witnessing the tragic way they lived, our hearts were moved.

It was a challenging time for the country as it faced an economic recession. Tourism was declining, and the United States was also grappling with its own financial downturn. Yet, we couldn't stand idly by. Inspired by the ideas passed down by my father, we decided to take action.

We began our mission by identifying appliance stores in areas where poor families resided. We made sure to focus only on those families who relied on welfare for support. To ensure the authenticity of their need, we enlisted the help of the city's welfare department to verify each family's situation. Once we had established the families' genuine need, we approached the stores and explained our plan.

Our goal was threefold: to help the stores by providing business during the economic downturn, to stimulate the economy by supporting local manufacturing of appliances, and most importantly, to offer a helping hand to those in need by giving them the much-needed appliances.

With our plan in motion, we negotiated with the stores to obtain the lowest possible prices. This way, we could stretch our resources and assist more families. As word spread about our mission, we gained support from unexpected quarters. Mayors from Jerusalem and Sderot, impressed by our efforts, recommended families that they believed qualified for assistance, and we gladly provided them as well with much-needed appliances.

The impact we had on these families was profound and heartwarming. Many of them couldn't believe that someone was willing to buy them a new washing machine, fridge, or oven. The shock and gratitude they expressed left us humbled and fulfilled. Their joy was palpable, with tears streaming down their faces as they blessed us for the unexpected generosity. Even the children couldn't contain their excitement, jumping up and down in sheer delight. We chose to remain anonymous, letting the families wonder about the identity of their benefactors.

In this endeavor, we were fortunate to have the support of David Schlesinger, the operator of Baruch U'Marpeh, an organization that provides free transportation for non-emergency medical issues. David played a crucial role in investigating each family's circumstances and negotiating fair prices. Initially, we offered to compensate him for his work, but he selflessly refused, considering his involvement as his own contribution to the cause. Witnessing the impact on these families, David, like us, was driven purely by a desire to alleviate the suffering of those in need.

As time went on, our efforts gained significant attention, and our program received widespread recognition. News of our endeavors spread through radio broadcasts across Israel. We still continue this philanthropic initiative annually, with each year bringing us renewed determination and a strengthened commitment to helping those less fortunate.

I personally visit many of these families, and I have taken my children and grandchildren to these homes to see the importance of this charitable work firsthand. I wanted them to comprehend the importance of compassion and the reality of poverty and low-paying jobs. The experience served as an educational lesson, encouraging them to pursue education and meaningful careers while nurturing empathy and understanding for those in need.

The reactions we received from the families we visited were diverse and touching. I remember one mother who couldn't stop crying as she baked her first cake in a new oven. Another family was overjoyed to have a functioning freezer, no longer having to worry about wasting food. And the children, their tears of happiness and gratitude, hugging us tightly, their innocent souls forever etched in our hearts.

The response from everyone involved was beyond our expectations.

The storekeepers were astounded by our compassion and commitment to making a difference in the lives of struggling families. The mayors and their staffs were moved by our acts of kindness and the news and radio people were left in awe, having never witnessed such a phenomenon of altruism before.

Our journey of giving had a lasting impact on the lives of many families and a profound effect on our own lives. It taught us the immense power of empathy and how a small act of kindness can create ripples of positive change in the world. This endeavor became a defining chapter in my life and strengthened my belief in the transformative power of charity and the human spirit.

But it also snowballed into a project that would reshape the lives of the ultra-Orthodox community in Israel. The ultra-Orthodox made up approximately 12 percent of the country's population, and sadly, most of them lived below the poverty line, with limited options and access to education. Their survival depended on charitable donations and government benefits, while many chose not to serve in the army.

Driven by a desire to find a solution to this predicament and to contribute positively to Israel, I came up with a plan that could offer employment opportunities while also addressing the challenges faced by the ultra-Orthodox community. The idea was relatively straightforward: to establish a computer class for ultra-Orthodox men, providing them with computer training and subsequently requiring them to serve in non-combat positions in the Israeli army. To put this plan into action, I secured a partnership with an AMIT school to house the classroom.

At first, AMIT refused to accept our donation that was conditioned on creating a Charedim-only computer science school. What changed their mind was a man by the name of Larry Blum, whose sister was married to my first cousin Perry. Larry knew the president of AMIT and was able to convince him to undertake this project. The result was one of the first programs in Israel to teach Charedim (men and women) computer science and cybersecurity.

I also faced significant opposition from the community's Rabbis and the men themselves. However, the support of the married women and mothers proved crucial, and with their backing, we pressed forward with the concept.

Our pilot project took root in the city of Petach Tikvah, where the students would spend half their day immersed in Torah studies and the other half learning computer science. After two years of training, the students underwent placement tests, with 60 percent joining the IDF in non-combat positions and 40 percent enlisting in non-combat positions in the air force.

The program's success surpassed all expectations, capturing the attention of the Israeli Air Force. Impressed with the students' caliber, the Air Force expressed a keen interest in recruiting more ultra-Orthodox men through our initiative. The officers took their enthusiasm to the Board of Education, urging them to support the expansion of similar schools like ours. The momentum grew, and even the Knesset, Israel's legislative body, was persuaded to contribute 1.4 million Israeli shekels toward the program's funding.

With the backing of the Knesset, the city of Petach Tikva generously donated land to build additional classrooms and dormitories dedicated to this degree program.

This revolutionary project aimed to transform 12 percent of the population from being reliant on handouts to becoming productive members of society, unlocking their untapped potential as a valuable resource for Israel's future.

And so, "The Charedi Revolution" was born.

Through perseverance and unwavering belief in our mission, we embarked on a journey to create lasting change in the lives of the ultra-Orthodox community, offering them a brighter and more self-sustaining future.

AFTERWORD

$\mathcal{A}$s I look back on my life's journey, I am filled with a profound sense of gratitude and wonder.

Throughout this memoir, I have shared numerous experiences, both triumphant and challenging, that have shaped who I am today. While some may attribute these occurrences to coincidence, fate, or mere luck, I firmly believe that there is a guiding force that orchestrates the events of our lives: Divine Providence.

Divine Providence, to me, is the hand of the Almighty God, subtly weaving the threads of our lives into a beautiful tapestry of experiences and opportunities. It is not something that occurs overnight or with immediate results. Instead, it is a process that unfolds over time, bringing about circumstances and encounters that eventually lead us to our destined path. In many instances, I can clearly see the hand of Divine Providence at work.

Each event, decision, and encounter was essential for me to take the next step in my journey. While others may have different interpretations, I am convinced that there was a higher plan guiding my life, a plan that required certain components to fall into place for me to seize the opportunities that presented themselves.

For example, reflecting on my various businesses, the people I met, the deals I made, and the transformations that occurred, I cannot deny the presence of Divine Providence. On many occasions, the synchronicity of events and the perfect alignment of circumstances were beyond ordinary explanation. It was as if unseen forces were working tirelessly to create a path uniquely tailored for me.

Furthermore, looking at historical narratives, we find countless instances of Divine Providence at play. The fulfillment of God's promise to Abraham, leading his descendants to their homeland, Israel, serves as a profound testament to the intricacies of Divine Providence. It took generations for the promise to be realized, a reminder that Divine Providence operates on its own timetable, far beyond our human understanding. The creation of the State of Israel, winning against four Arab armies, stunned the world.

In my own life, as the first Orthodox mayor ever elected in the USA, the creation of the *eruv* stands as a testament to Divine Providence. Countless factors had to align and a series of events had to unfold for this project to become a reality. It was as though the hand of God was paving the way for this historical endeavor.

As a trial attorney, I have to end my story with a closing argument to my jury: you, the reader. I have been truthful in the chronicling of the events of my life and how they occurred. I have the privilege of hindsight to see that the most important, life-changing events occurred because of forces beyond my comprehension. I look at these points and am amazed at the interconnectedness of them. Some seem insignificant: I kicked my Rabbi, I was sent to public school, I shined shoes on the streets, I won a trip to Cuba, and I was on probation in school. The way I met my future wife, the way I passed school, passed the bar, found those paintings in Europe – the list is as long as this memoir, each event unfolding in what can only be described as something otherworldly.

Keeping the Sabbath was critical for two major points in my life as well. If I hadn't kept the Sabbath when I was in law school and had taken the test on Saturday, I would likely have never graduated law school. Sitting in Professor Kuvin's home on that Sunday, discovering the connection to his grandfather in a picture that sat on his mantle, and then receiving two As was the setup for the rest of my life. Likewise, Joe Malek came to my synagogue to ask me not to run for office solely because I was a Sabbath observer and would affect his ability to win. My keeping Sabbath made me a threat to him then but it also created the relationship that made sure I would win years later.

As I conclude this memoir, I want to encourage you, the reader, to look back on each of the events I have described and embrace the concept of Divine Providence in their own lives. While we may not always understand the intricacies of the grand plan, we can trust that every experience, whether joyous or challenging, serves a purpose in shaping us into who we are meant to be. Divine Providence gently nudges us along our journey, guiding us toward the fulfillment of our purpose and the realization of our dreams.

Let us remain open to the signs, seize the opportunities, and trust that in the tapestry of life, Divine Providence is the master weaver, skillfully crafting a story that is uniquely ours. As we navigate the uncertainties of the future, may we find solace in knowing that we are not alone in our journey and that Divine Providence is always at work, even when we are unaware of its presence. With this newfound understanding, may we embrace life's twists and turns with faith and hope, confident that the hand of the Divine is guiding us towards a fulfilling and purposeful life.

ACKNOWLEDGMENTS

I WOULD LIKE TO EXPRESS MY DEEP GRATITUDE TO THE people who have made a profound impact on my life, shaping my journey in various ways.

I was fortunate to connect with three fellow students who became my law partners.

I can honestly say that in 35 years together we really never had any personal arguments. We had the normal heated discussions about issues related to our practice, but we always resolved them in a friendly way.

My partners Sherwin Stauber, a practicing Rabbi, and Bob Grover both became municipal judges. My partner Marvin Weinstein was elected Mayor of Surfside, and the minute he found a house he liked in Miami Beach, he resigned and left Surfside to live in Miami Beach. I really never understood that decision, but he bought a magnificent home that my wife found for him. My partner Bob Grover surprised me when he slowly became serious about observing the laws of a religious Jew. His wife, Elaine, became an active woman in the community, participating in many religious activities.

I owe all of them a thank you beyond words as they helped me in all my activities including three actual elections which we never thought we would win. They encouraged me to accept the judgeship offered to me by the governor of Florida, and I presided there for over two years before returning to our law practice. It was a wonderful and exciting 35-year experience.

I met some talented men who became not only helpful but extremely close friends.

Bob Goodman had an unusual gift in understanding how to have our message in the campaign presented to the public and developed some great slogans. Best of all he had such confidence in me that he agreed to handle my first campaign for free. I will never forget when he said, "I trust you and you will make it up to me someday." I then helped him get elected to the Miami Beach Commission.

Dr. Paul Glassman gave me my first and largest donation and over the next 60 years patched me up every time I needed medical treatment.

My oldest and best friend, Dr. Tepper, was always there to say okay to whatever I proposed and because of that nature he was responsible for me finding all the sources for my father's business in Europe. We shared a lifetime of unusual experiences, from sail fishing in Mexico to meeting Menachem Begin in Israel.

All four of us are now retired, and thank God we are still able to enjoy our family and friends in fairly good health.

My heartfelt thanks go to my childhood friend, Marty Brown, who selflessly gave me his life savings when I was 21 to cover my first year of law school. His support was invaluable, and I am forever grateful.

To Stuart Rubin, with whom I shared countless hunting adventures from the age of 16 and remained in constant touch throughout our lives, I am grateful for the enduring friendship and for his hosting me and my family at his mountain hotel for many years! I am proud to see him become one of the most successful businessmen in the city of Hendersonville, North Carolina.

I must also acknowledge Charles Fridman, whose parents fought in the French underground during the war. I am grateful that I was able to organize a bar mitzvah for him at the Kotel when he was in his fifties!

My dear friend, Jack Burstein, a very strategic thinking CPA, played a pivotal role in guiding me toward various impactful projects. Jack's suggestion to contribute to Bar Ilan University in Israel set us on a path of philanthropy that led to the establishment of an engineering lab for research and the subsequent donation of lecture halls, hospital rooms, computer centers, robotic centers, welcome centers, and more to institutions like Hadassah and Shaare Zedek hospitals, AMIT and Emunah schools, and many other deserving organizations in Israel and South Florida.

My younger brother, Mel, has been a constant presence in my life. Despite our childhood squabbles, our bond only grew stronger with time. I remember advising him to attend college in Miami instead of going up North, and I am proud of his incredible achievements. Going to Miami was a good choice as he wound up winning a major scholarship to NYU where he earned a Ph.D. in Mathematics. He went on to work for prestigious institutions like the National Science Foundation. His wife, Barbara, became a successful real estate saleswoman, and their harmonious relationship for over 50 years is a testament to their love. As I write this note, we are about to celebrate the holidays together in Israel, a testament to our enduring family bond.

Marcia Sage, my wife's sister and her partner for 47 years, is a steady, reliable, and capable individual who, as a single mother, raised her daughter Morgan to become a successful woman. Marcia is an astute businesswoman who can make successful business decisions in under a minute. She is a respected and loving member of the entire family, and I am proud of her.

Joan was not only a great campaigner in all three of my campaigns, but is also a devoted wife, mother to our three boys, and the hardest working grandmother. There is not a day that goes by that she doesn't communicate with one or more of our grandchildren, regardless of whether they are in New York, Miami, or Israel. I am in awe of the devotion that they all have to each other. As my partner in life, she has been by my side through good times and bad times, always a dependable, caring, and loving wife. She is also entitled to a purple heart as she survived so many different episodes in listening and correcting many of my different experiences as this book was brought to life. I thank her beyond any words that appear in a dictionary.

As for our three sons, I am so proud of each of them.

Ivan and Jason became attorneys, and while neither one practices law, they both went on to build independent businesses. Avi successfully operates the largest jewelry store in the Catskill Mountains and has become an international writer, lecturer, and author on religious matters. He is educating the younger generation and has been well received in schools and colleges in the U.S. and Israel. He also is the one who gave me the original idea for this book and who kept encouraging me until he finally convinced me to write it both for our family and for the eventual reader who may benefit from the lessons I learned along the way.

I especially want to thank his wife Adina who came to my rescue after several professional writers didn't work out. Adina brought with her a very unusual and admirable expertise in helping me to better express my stories along with their religious undertones. She always managed to strike the right note with her keen sensitivity to nuance.

I want to thank my son Jason who flew to Miami Beach multiple times to interview me in depth about my life experiences and for connecting me with Tzvi Mauer from Urim Publications and Ktav Publishing House.

All my children support organizations in the United States and Israel as well as participate in programs to benefit the Jewish community and Israel. Each of them has raised their children in the same manner they were raised. They have been devoted, caring children and have made sure that all their children are actively involved in family matters. That in itself is a miracle for our family. More importantly, they help each other and support Joan and me on any and all of our projects.

In closing, I want to share the story of King Solomon, one of the wisest individuals. Despite achieving all his desires, he came to the realization that chasing worldly things like honor, money, and fame is like trying to grasp the wind. When you open your hand, you realize it is full of nothingness. Rather than catching the wind, his conclusion is to fear God, keep His commandments, and stay close to one's family. This resonates deeply with me.

I hope that my story will inspire others to believe in Divine Providence.

ABOUT THE AUTHOR

NORMAN CIMENT'S DIVERSE CAREER ENCOMPASSES LAW, mediation, politics, real estate, and philanthropy, all deeply influenced by his Orthodox Jewish faith. Educated at the University of Miami, he embarked on a legal career before entering politics. In 1967, he was elected to the Miami Beach city commission, and in 1971, he was appointed as a state judge by the governor. In 1981, he broke new ground by being elected in Miami Beach as the first Orthodox Jewish mayor of a major U.S. city and then building the first *eruv* in Florida.

After retiring from his legal practice, he became a prominent mediator, real estate syndicator, and philanthropist focused on charities in Miami Beach and Israel. He pioneered a cyber-education degree program for Charedim in the IDF; created VouchersForLife.com to provide gift certificates from Israeli businesses to victims of terror; and started giveafridge.com to donate Israeli-made appliances to needy families. He is also on the Board of Governors at Tel Aviv University.

Alongside his wife, Joan, Norman's family life, which includes their three sons and their families, remains central to his legacy of service and communal contribution.